Kurt Bangert

Wirtschaftsenglisch für den Berufseinstieg

2., überarbeitete und erweiterte Auflage

UVK Verlag · München

Umschlagabbildung: © SolStock · iStock
Autorenfoto (S. 2): © privat

Bibliografische Information der Deutschen Nationalbibliothek
Die Deutsche Nationalbibliothek verzeichnet diese Publikation in der Deutschen Nationalbibliografie; detaillierte bibliografische Daten sind im Internet über http://dnb.dnb.de abrufbar.

2. Auflage 2021
1. Auflage 2015

– ein Unternehmen der Narr Francke Attempto Verlag GmbH + Co. KG
Dischingerweg 5 · D-72070 Tübingen

Internet: www.narr.de
eMail: info@narr.de

Einbandgestaltung: Atelier Reichert, Stuttgart
CPI books GmbH, Leck

utb-Nr. 4294
ISBN 978-3-8252-5674-6 (Print)
ISBN 978-3-8385-5674-1 (ePDF)
ISBN 978-3-8463-5674-6 (ePUB)

My sincere thanks go to Maggie and David Wilford (Myddle, England) for proofreading the material and for their practical suggestions.
I would also like to express my gratitude to my colleague, Prof. Jackie Pocklington (Stahnsdorf), for his valuable advice on Unit 9.

KB

Vorwort

Lieber Berufseinsteiger, liebe Berufseinsteigerin,

Sie haben in der Schule, während der Berufsausbildung oder an der Hochschule (Wirtschafts-)Englisch gelernt und nun Ihre erste Stelle angetreten. Jetzt wird es ernst: Der erste Telefonanruf von englischsprachigen Geschäftspartnern lässt nicht lange auf sich warten. Wie begrüße ich die Anruferin noch mal? Was sage ich, wenn ich sie nicht richtig verstanden habe? Wie verabschiede ich mich professionell?

Der vorliegende „Kompaktkurs Wirtschaftsenglisch für den Berufseinstieg" hilft Ihnen, sich optimal auf diese und andere Herausforderungen des beruflichen Alltags vorzubereiten. In kleinen, überschaubaren Kapiteln haben wir für Sie die Vokabeln, Ausdrücke und Redewendungen zusammengestellt, die Sie für die Kommunikation mit Ihrem Geschäftspartner oder Ihrer Geschäftspartnerin aus dem Ausland benötigen. Dabei haben wir uns auf Situationen konzentriert, die Sie mit hoher Wahrscheinlichkeit regelmäßig im Berufsleben antreffen werden. So stellen Sie z. B. Ihr Unternehmen auf Englisch vor, Sie telefonieren oder verhandeln mit Ihren Geschäftspartnern in der Fremdsprache, Sie schreiben Briefe und E-Mails oder präsentieren ein Produkt vor internationalem Publikum. Gut möglich, dass Sie ein Meeting in englischer Sprache moderieren müssen oder sich auf eine Stelle auf Englisch bewerben möchten. Auch hierfür finden Sie die passenden Vokabeln und Wendungen.

Die Kapitel sind so aufgebaut, dass Sie zunächst einen Musterdialog oder eine Musterpräsentation lesen und danach die wesentlichen sprachlichen Mittel dazu mit Hilfe einer übersichtlichen Tabelle lernen können. Jedes Kapitel beinhaltet zudem einige Hinweise auf Besonderheiten des jeweiligen Themas. Damit Sie die neuen Vokabeln und Ausdrücke trainieren können, schließt jedes Kapitel mit einigen Übungen ab. Mit Hilfe des Schlüssels im Anhang des Büchleins können Sie überprüfen, ob Sie alle Aufgaben richtig gelöst haben.

Das Material wird ergänzt durch Tipps und Strategien zum eigenständigen Sprachenlernen und einer Auswahlbibliographie mit Büchern und Links, die sich für das Englischlernen als sehr hilfreich herausgestellt haben (z. B. Hinweise auf Wörterbücher, Wortschatztraining, Grammatiktraining und Online-Ressourcen).

Wir hoffen, dass Ihnen der Kompaktkurs ein nützlicher Begleiter für Ihren Berufseinstieg sein wird.

Berlin, im Dezember 2020 Prof. Dr. Kurt Bangert

Inhalt

1 Kontakte knüpfen [Making Contacts]

1.1 Beispieldialog

Rob Long:	Hello, I don't think we've met. Robert Long.
Fiona Newby:	Fiona Newby. Pleased to meet you.
Rob:	And what company are you from, Ms Newby?
Fiona:	PaperWorks. We produce and sell high-quality paper for the printing industry. I'm the sales manager for this region.
Rob:	PaperWorks … I've heard about your company. Your business is growing very rapidly at the moment, in spite of the difficult times.
Fiona:	Yes, we're doing quite well. And what about you? Who do you work for, Mr Long?
Rob:	Please call me Rob. I'm the managing director of a large consulting company. We offer our services mainly to the printing industry. Here's my card.
Fiona:	Thanks, Rob. And here's mine.
	Another person is joining the group.
Rob:	Fiona, may I introduce you to a colleague? This is Martin Miller. He's one of our consulting specialists. Martin, please meet Fiona Newby. She's here for PaperWorks.
Martin:	How do you do?
Fiona:	Pleased to meet you.
Rob:	Fiona, I'm sure Martin would like to hear more about your company … If you two would excuse me for a minute …

1.2 Wortschatz

sich mit jemandem bekannt machen	Hello, I don't think we've met. / Hello, my name is … How do you do? / Pleased to meet you.
jemanden vorstellen	I'd like to introduce you to … May I introduce you to …? I'd like you to meet … / Please meet … Martin, this is … He / she works for … Martin, have you met …? He / she works for …
nach dem beruflichen Hintergrund fragen	What company are you from, Mr … / Mrs … / Ms … ? Who do you work for?
jemandem den Gebrauch des Vornamens anbieten	Please call me Rob / Fiona. I'm Rob / Fiona.
Visitenkarten austauschen	Here's my card. And here's mine.
Auskunft über die Firma geben	We're a production company. We produce / manufacture parts for the … industry. We're in the consulting / … business. We offer services to … I work for myself. / I'm self-employed.

1.3 Tipps

- Um sich auf Englisch vorzustellen, verwenden Sie in der Regel feststehende Ausdrücke / Phrasen. Auf „How do you do?“ bei einem ersten Kennenlernen beispielsweise antworten Sie ebenfalls mit „How do you do?“ oder „Pleased to meet you.“ Unangebracht wäre es hingegen, auf die Wendung „How do you do?“ über das eigene Befinden zu berichten. Bei wiederholten Treffen verwenden Sie bitte eher Wendungen wie „How are you?“, „How is it going?“ oder „How are things?“.
- In der englischsprachigen Welt reden sich Geschäftspartner oft schon nach einem ersten kurzen Austausch mit dem Vornamen an. Dies ist keinesfalls mit freundschaftlicher Nähe zu verwechseln; das Gespräch wird weiterhin professionell geführt, wenn auch in einer weniger gezwungenen Atmosphäre. Sollten Sie mit dem Geschäftspartner zu einem späteren Zeitpunkt auch ein Gespräch auf Deutsch führen können, stolpern Sie nicht in eine interkulturelle Falle: Der Gebrauch des Vornamens hat in der Geschäftswelt mit Duzen nichts zu tun. Bleiben Sie beim Vornamen, aber nur in Verbindung mit „Sie“.
- Wenn Sie Visitenkarten austauschen, stecken Sie die Karte Ihres Gegenübers nicht einfach in die Tasche. Nehmen Sie sie bewusst wahr (Name, Firma, Position) und zeigen Sie so Wertschätzung. Dies gilt insbesondere bei Kontaktaufnahme zu asiatischen Geschäftspartnern.
- Noch ein Wort zum „Handshaking“: Im englischsprachigen Raum geben Sie sich beim ersten Kennenlernen und bei einem Wiedersehen nach längerer Zeit die Hand. Das Händeschütteln vor regelmäßig stattfindenden Besprechungen oder im täglichen Umgang mit Kollegen, wie es in Deutschland häufig vorkommt, ist unüblich.

1.4 Übungen

Exercise 1

The following scrambled words are all from Unit 1. Can you identify the originals?

1. LSPEDEA ______
2. COAYPNM ______
3. ODUERCP ______
4. IUSENSSB ______
5. SSREVCIE ______
6. TRSCUDPO ______
7. DTNURISY ______
8. GUECEAOLL ______
9. NRCDOUIET ______
10. LSFE-PYEEMDLO ______

Exercise 2

Match each phrase from the left to the correct expression on the right.

1. Hello, I don't think we've met.	a. Fine! It's actually close to the city center.
2. Here's my card.	b. Unfortunately we need to get back to London tomorrow.
3. What do you specialize in?	c. Yeah, a bit bumpy, but otherwise fine.
4. Did you have a good flight?	d. Please call me Fiona.
5. Nice to meet you, Ms Newby.	e. That's a good idea. Why not meet at Michelino's on Thursday at one?

6. Who do you work for?
7. How's your hotel?
8. How about lunch one day next week?
9. What do you do for a living?
10. Are you staying for a few days?

f. No, my name's Ian Jones, from InterSpecs. How do you do?
g. Southview Publishers, the market leader in virtual learning.
h. Thank you. And here's mine.
i. We manufacture parts for the car industry.
j. I'm in sales.

The correct matching is 1___, 2___, 3___, 4___, 5___, 6___, 7___, 8___, 9 ___, 10 ___.

Exercise 3

Wie fragen Sie auf Englisch, ob …

1. Ihre Geschäftspartnerin Ihre Firma gut finden konnte?

   ____

2. Sie etwas zu trinken anbieten können?

   ____

3. sie zum ersten Mal in Berlin ist?

   ____

4. sie Zeit haben wird, sich etwas in der Stadt umzuschauen?

   ____

5. Sie zum Geschäftlichen übergehen sollen?

   ____

2 Über das Unternehmen, Produkte und Dienstleistungen sprechen [Talking about Companies, Products and Services]

2.1 Beispielpräsentation 1

"I work in the purchasing department of a manufacturing company called CarTech. We produce parts for the car industry. We have three branches, two of which are based in Germany, one in Poland. Our company was founded in 1995 by Erik Miller, who still is the managing director. We are one of the market leaders; our main competitors are located in the southern part of Germany. We specialize in high-tech cylinder heads (*Zylinderköpfe*). Other products include pistons (*Kolben*) and piston rings (*Kolbenringe*). Our company has about 200 employees. Most of them work in production, others in administration and sales. We have a turnover of roughly 75 million euros per year. The headquarter of our company is in Munich."

2.2 Beispielpräsentation 2

"I'd like to talk about the company's departments. There are six units in all, and here's what they deal with. The **management** ensures that the company reaches its strategic goals and provides leadership to the employees. The **research & development** department (R&D) develops high-tech components which are then produced in our factory. The **purchasing department** procures all the materials needed for production or the daily operation of the company. The **accounts department** is in charge of all incoming and outgoing payments. The **HR depart-**

ment looks after the employees' needs and takes on new staff. The **marketing & sales department** advertises the new products and makes sure that the products find their way to the customer. Because sales people are in close contact with their customers, they are able to provide the company with important market information."

2.3 Wortschatz

Aktivitäten (in) einer Firma beschreiben	
to found / set up / start a company	eine Firma gründen
a start-up company	eine Neugründung, ein Jungunternehmen
the CEO / Managing Director (MD) / founder / owner of a company / entrepreneur [ˌɒntrəprəˈnɜː]	der Vorstandsvorsitzende / Geschäftsführer / Gründer / Inhaber einer Firma / Unternehmer
the MD ensures that the company reaches its strategic goals	der Geschäftsführer stellt sicher, dass die Firma ihre strategischen Ziele erreicht
the company is located / based in Berlin / the company's headquarter is in Berlin / the company is Berlin-based	die Firma hat ihren Sitz in Berlin
the company has branches / subsidiaries in …	die Firma hat Niederlassungen / Tochtergesellschaften in …
the company employs 150 people / has 150 employees / staff	die Firma beschäftigt 150 Mitarbeiter
the company is privately owned (LTD = limited company) / publically owned (PLC=public corporation) / government-owned	die Firma ist eine private GmbH / eine Aktiengesellschaft / ein staatliches Unternehmen

the company makes / produces / manufactures ... / the company's core business fields are ... / offers a wide range of products	die Firma stellt ... her / produziert ... / die Kern geschäftsfelder der Firma sind ... / bietet eine breite Produktpalette an
the company provides services to ...	die Firma bietet Dienstleistungen für ... an
we specialize in ...	wir sind auf ... spezialisiert
to export to / to import from	exportieren nach / importieren aus / von
wholesalers sell business-to-business (b2b), retailers sell to consumers (b2c)	Großhändler beliefern Firmenkunden, Einzelhändler verkaufen an Privatkunden
to run a franchise business / franchisee / franchisor	ein Franchise-Geschäft betreiben / Franchise-Nehmer / Franchise-Geber
the company has a turnover of ... euros per year / to make a profit / loss of ...	die Firma macht einen Umsatz von ... pro Jahr / einen Gewinn / Verlust in Höhe von ... machen

Positionen und Aktivitäten von Angestellten beschreiben

to work in the production department / in production / in the sales department / in sales	in der Produktionsabteilung / in der Produktion / in der Vertriebsabteilung / im Vertrieb arbeiten
to run a company / a department	eine Firma / eine Abteilung leiten
to procure materials	Material beschaffen
to be in charge of / to be responsible for / to deal with	für etwas zuständig / verantwortlich sein / sich um etwas kümmern
his job involves a lot of travel / customer contact	seine Aufgabe beinhaltet viel Reisetätigkeit / Kundenkontakt
to report directly to the MD	dem Geschäftsführer direkt unterstellt sein / berichten

Abteilungen einer Firma benennen	
the management	die Geschäftsführung
research & development (R&D) department	die Forschungs- und Entwicklungsabteilung
purchasing department	Einkaufsabteilung
accounts department	Buchhaltung
HR / human resources department	Personalabteilung
marketing & sales department	Marketing- und Vertriebsabteilung
legal department	Rechtsabteilung

2.4 Tipps

Viele Gespräche auf internationalen Kongressen oder Messen beginnen mit der Frage nach den Aktivitäten Ihres Unternehmens und Ihrer eigenen Zuständigkeit. Schön, wenn Sie dann sprachlich souverän agieren können. Nehmen Sie sich die Zeit und stellen Sie Ihre eigene kleine „Präsentation" zusammen; die Ausdrücke in diesem Kapitel können Ihnen dabei helfen.

- Wenn es heißt „What do you do for a living?" („Was machen Sie beruflich?"), könnten Sie z. B. einfach antworten „I'm in sales", Sie sind im Vertrieb tätig. Das reicht fürs Erste vollständig, warten Sie ab, wie sich das Gespräch entwickelt.
- Nutzen Sie „customers" für Kunden, die handfeste Produkte / Waren („products / goods") einkaufen, „clients" für alle, die Dienstleistungen („services") in Anspruch nehmen. Etwa: „We are retailers and offer a wide range of goods to our customers". Aber: „Our clients expect a first-class consultancy service."
- Achtung, falscher Freund: Das englische Wort „branch" bedeutet in der Geschäftswelt „Zweigstelle, Niederlassung". Das deutsche Wort „Branche" hingegen wird mit „business" oder „industry" wiedergegeben. So sagen Sie z. B. „I work in the insurance business / industry." Viele weitere Falsche Freunde finden Sie in Kapitel 10.

2.5 Übungen

Exercise 1

Describing job responsibilities. Fill in the missing phrases.

1. I work in the HR department. I ____________________ of all the company's interns.
2. I ____________________ with overseas customers over the phone.
3. I ____________________ in research and development. We are in the process of developing a brand-new device.
4. I'm in the ____________________. We ____________ ____________________ the firm's supplies, i. e. everything that is necessary to run the company.

Exercise 2

Word families will help you to expand your vocabulary. Collect verbs, nouns, adjectives and adverbs from word fields below. The first one has been done for you.

1. production
   production (n.)
   product (n.)
   producer (n.)
   produce (n., used for food)
   to produce sthg. (v.)
   productive (adj., e. g. staff)
2. special

   ____

   ____

   ____

____

____

____

____

3. employment

____

____

____

____

4. innovation

____

____

____

____

Exercise 3

Match the words from the two columns that have a similar meaning.

1. establish oneself in a market	a. expansion
2. manufacturer	b. provide with
3. production site	c. look for business partners in the region
4. search for local suppliers	d. open a company in a certain area
5. growth	e. producer
6. work with	f. plant
7. supply	g. collaborate

The correct matching is 1___, 2___, 3___, 4___, 5___, 6___, 7___.

3 Auf Englisch telefonieren [Telephoning in English]

3.1 Beispieldialog

Receptionist:	Good morning, ABC Photo Publishing, how can I help you?
Caller:	Hello, I'd like to speak to Nick Millibrand, please.
Receptionist:	Who's calling, please?
Caller:	This is John Sledgehammer from Pre-Press Enterprises.
Receptionist:	Thank you. Putting you through now, Mr Sledgehammer.
Sledgehammer:	Thank you.
Millibrand:	Nick Millibrand speaking.
Sledgehammer:	Hello, Mr Millibrand. This is John Sledgehammer from Pre-Press Enterprises.
Millibrand:	Oh, hello, Mr Sledgehammer. What can I do for you?
Sledgehammer:	Well, the reason I'm calling is to find out about the photos we ordered one month ago. They are now two weeks overdue and we need them urgently for production.
Millibrand:	I'm sorry to hear that, Mr Sledgehammer. One moment, I'll just have to get the file. Would you please hold the line? … *music, one minute later* … Sorry to keep you waiting, Mr Sledgehammer. Something seems to have gone wrong with the delivery. I'll have to get in contact with the courier. Can I get back to you on this?
Sledgehammer:	Yes, no problem. When will I hear from you again?

3

Millibrand:	By the end of the day at the latest. I apologize for the delay. Thank you for calling, Mr Sledgehammer.
Sledgehammer:	Thank you and goodbye for now.
Millibrand:	Goodbye and have a nice day.

3.2 Wortschatz

das Gespräch annehmen	Good morning / afternoon, ABC Photo Publishing, can I help you / how may I help you?
Anrufer sucht den richtigen Gesprächspartner	I'd like to speak to … / Could I speak to …, please? Would you please put me through to …?
den Anrufer identifizieren	Who's calling please? May I ask who's calling?
der Anrufer stellt sich vor	This is John Sledgehammer from Pre-Press Enterprises. It's Helen Wood speaking.
den Anrufer durchstellen	I'll put you through. Putting you through now. You're through now.
den Anrufer um Geduld bitten	I'm sorry the line is engaged / busy. Will you wait / hold? I'm sorry he's / she's in a meeting. Would you like to leave a message? I'm sorry, he's / she's out of the office at the moment. Can he / she call you back?
den Grund für den Anruf nennen	The reason I'm calling is to find out about … I'm calling / phoning to ask / find out about … I need to talk to someone in accounts.

auf das Problem des Anrufers eingehen	One moment, sir / madam / Mr … / Ms …, I'll just have to get the file. OK, let me check this for you on my computer. Ah, yes, here we are. We sent out the photos last Friday. I need to check this with my colleague first. Can I get back to you?
sich verabschieden	Well, thanks a lot. Bye for now. Goodbye, sir / madam. Thanks for calling. Goodbye. Goodbye and have a nice day.
schlechte Verbindung	I'm afraid the line is very bad. Could you speak up please? Sorry, I didn't catch that. Could you say it again, please? I'm afraid I can't hear you.
Besonderheiten	Das Handy heißt auf Englisch „mobile phone" (GB) oder „cell phone" (US), niemals „handy", was „praktisch, handlich" bedeutet. Aussprache von Telefonnummern: 0044 573 83 95: double oh – double four – five-seven-three – eight-three – nine-five. Anstatt „oh" [əʊ] hört man auch häufig „zero" [ˈzɪərəʊ].

3.3 Tipps

Telefonieren in der Fremdsprache ist eine besondere Herausforderung, Sie sind völlig auf Ihr Hörverstehen angewiesen, können sich nicht durch die Körpersprache (Mimik, Gestik) des Gegenübers helfen lassen; außerdem müssen Sie sich blitzschnell auf unerwartete Akzente / Dialekte einstellen. Deswegen ist die Vorbereitung aufs Gespräch umso wichtiger:

- Halten Sie Stift und Notizblock bereit.
- Rechnen Sie damit, dass Ihr Geschäftspartner sehr schnell spricht („That was a bit too fast. Could you repeat it, please?").
- Stellen Sie sicher, dass Sie alles richtig verstanden haben („If I understand you correctly, … / May I summarize what we have just said?").
- Formulieren Sie stets höflich: Lieber ein „thank you" oder „please" zu viel als zu wenig.
- Führen Sie wichtige Gespräche wegen der stabileren Verbindung möglichst vom Festnetz, nicht vom Mobiltelefon.
- Spielen Sie wichtige Gespräche vorher einmal sprachlich durch; Sie werden merken, das steigert Ihr Selbstvertrauen.

3.4 Übungen

Exercise 1

Find at least one typical phrase for each of the following telephone situations.

1. Introducing yourself

   ____

2. Asking who is on the telephone

   ____

3. Asking for someone

   ____

4. Connecting someone

   ____

5. How to reply when someone is not available

   ____

6. Taking a message

   ____

7. Finishing the conversation politely

Exercise 2

Read the (very impolite) dialogue below and try to improve it, using the telephone expressions you have learned.

Receptionist	**Caller**
1. MasterMind Ltd. What's up?	2. I want to speak to Chris Clever.
3. No chance, he's busy. Any message you want to leave?	4. Yes. I'm Duncan Dumble, tell him to ring me asap.
5. Didn't get your last name. Spell it.	6. D-U-M-B-L-E
7. Okeydoke. Will give message to him later.	8. Thanks. CU.
9. Cheers.	

Exercise 3

The following statements are answers (A) to questions (Q) that someone asks on the phone. Using the telephone phrases you have learned, try to find out what the questions are.

1. Q.: ______________________________

A.: Yes, I'd like to speak to Benedict Miller, please.

2. Q.: ______________________________

A. This is Ariana Field from SmartyDigy.

3. Q.: ______________________________

A.: Well, the reason for my call is to find out about …

4. Q.: ______________________________

A.: I'm sorry, Alan is in a meeting.

5. Q.: ______________________________

A.: Yes, of course. Is that better?

4 Geschäftsbriefe und E-Mails schreiben [Writing Business Letters and E-Mails]

4.1 Beispielbrief

The Business Letter (British Layout)

Schnell-Verlag GmbH
Schnellstr. 25 ①
15345 Berlin
Tel. +49 30 24425665
Fax. +49 30 24425666
E-Mail: heiser@schnellverlag.com
www.schnellverlag.com

HH / OW ②
2 April 20XX ③

The Export Manager
Printing Unlimited ④
18 South View Road
Chester
SY5 7JH
Great Britain

Dear Sir or Madam ⑤

Request for Information about your Printing Services ⑥

We visited your stand at the London Print Fair and were most impressed by the technology you demonstrated, together ⑦ with your colleagues from your subsidiary in Hong Kong. As a leading publisher in the area of non-fiction with an expanding list, we are looking for printing partners outside Europe, preferably in Asia. We are enclosing our latest company brochure.

Please send us more detailed information on your printing services and also some samples that can demonstrate your quality standard. Can you guarantee prompt delivery from Hong Kong to Europe? Information on your terms of payment and delivery and all discounts granted would also be appreciated.

Should you require a reference, please contact Deutsche Bank in Berlin. If your offer meets our requirements, we will be pleased to place a trial order with you.

We look forward to hearing from you soon. ——— ⑧

Yours faithfully ——— ⑨
Schnell-Verlag GmbH

Hannes Heiser
Purchasing Director ——— ⑩

Enc ——— ⑪

Cc: Fritz Fuchs, Project Manager ——— ⑫

4.2 Wortschatz

request for information / quotation	Informationsanforderung / Angebotsaufforderung
to visit a stand / be impressed by …	einen Messestand besuchen / beeindruckt sein von …
as a leading publisher / company	als führender Verlag / führendes Unternehmen
to look for partners / enclose brochures / leaflets / flyers	Geschäftspartner suchen / Broschüren / Faltblätter / Flyer beilegen

to send detailed information on / about … / samples	genaue Informationen über … zukommen lassen / Muster schicken
to guarantee prompt delivery	schnelle Lieferung garantieren / zusagen
terms of payment and delivery	Zahlungs- und Lieferbedingungen
to grant discounts	Rabatte / Preisnachlässe gewähren
Information on … would be appreciated.	Wir sind dankbar für Informationen über …
to require a reference	eine Bankreferenz verlangen
If your offer meets our requirements …	Wenn Ihr Angebot unseren Anforderungen entspricht …
to place a trial order	eine Probebestellung aufgeben
We look forward to hearing from you soon.	Wir freuen uns darauf, bald von Ihnen zu hören.
Sales / Purchasing / Marketing Director	Verkaufs- / Einkaufs- / Marketingleiter

4.3 Tipps

① Briefkopf (**letter head**) mit Firmenlogo und Kontaktdaten.

② Bezugszeichen (**reference initials**). Das Bezugszeichen besteht im Englischen häufig aus den Initialen des Autors (HH: Hannes Heiser) und ggf. auch der Schreibkraft (OW: Oskar Winter).

③ Es gibt verschiedene akzeptable Datumsangaben (**date**). Am einfachsten und universellsten ist die hier verwendete: Ziffer für den Tag plus ausgeschriebener Monat plus 4-stellige Jahresangabe. Keine Satzzeichen verwenden.

④ Empfängeradresse (**receiver's address**). Im vorliegenden Fall hat der Autor keinen namentlich bekannten Ansprechpartner, er möchte den Exportmanager erreichen.

⑤ Anrede (**salutation**). Ohne namentlich bekannten Ansprechpartner verwenden Sie bitte „Dear Sir or Madam" / „Dear Sir / Madam". Reden Sie Geschäftspartnerinnen immer mit dem neutralen „Ms" {mɪz} an, also „Dear Ms Wood". Empfehlung: Setzen Sie weder ein Komma hinter die Anrede noch hinter die Schlussformel (⑨). Im Amerikanischen sind Kommas an diesen Stellen allerdings üblich.

⑥ Die Betreffzeile (**subject line**) wird unterstrichen oder fett formatiert, die Schlüsselwörter zudem mit großen Anfangsbuchstaben geschrieben. Eine Besonderheit: In britischen Geschäftsbriefen folgt die Betreffzeile der Anrede, im Amerikanischen ist es umgekehrt, also wie im Deutschen.

⑦ Der Hauptteil des Briefes (**body of the letter**) beginnt **immer** mit einem Großbuchstaben und enthält alle relevanten Informationen. Beachten Sie den Briefstil: klar, direkt, höflich. Formulieren Sie Ihren Geschäftsbrief so, dass für den Empfänger deutlich wird, was als nächstes zu tun ist. Geschäftsbriefe enthalten Wendungen / Standardausdrücke, die Sie immer wieder verwenden können.

⑧ Höfliche Schlussformulierung (**polite ending**), oft eine Standardformulierung.

⑨ Schlussformel (**complimentary close**). Hannes Heiser wählt „Yours faithfully", weil er den Adressaten nicht namentlich kennt, andernfalls würde er „Yours sincerely" benutzen. Im Amerikanischen passt „Sincerely," in den meisten Fällen.

⑩ Platzieren Sie Ihre Position (**job title**) unterhalb Ihres Namens.

⑪ Anlage (**Enclosure** [Enc]). Zu verwenden, wenn Sie Ihrem Brief Infomaterialien wie Broschüren oder Prospekte beilegen.

⑫ Kopie („**cc**" für „carbon copy", stammt von dem heute kaum noch bekannten Durchschlagpapier). Wird genutzt, um den Vorgesetzten oder einen Kollegen über den Vorgang zu informieren.

4.4 Beispiel-E-Mail

An... j.prior@prinunlim.com

Cc...

Senden

Betreff: Sample Material and Print Fair next week

Dear John

Thanks for sending us the sample material. My first reaction is that we can use it but I'm going to have a closer look together with our specialists and get back to you on this asap.
Concerning the meeting at the Print Fair in London next week, I'm afraid I won't be able to make it. I'll be traveling for the rest of the month. But Joanna will be happy to discuss the new project with you. Come and see her at our stand.

Kind regards

Hannes

Hannes Heiser
Purchasing Director
Schnell Verlag GmbH

j.prior@prinunlim.com

4.5 Tipps

Im Unterschied zum Geschäftsbrief weist die E-Mail folgende Merkmale auf. Sie

- ist das Standard-Kommunikationsmittel im täglichen Geschäftsverkehr.
- hat eine kurze, prägnante Betreffzeile (subject line), die den Empfänger auf einen Blick darüber informiert, worum es in der Mail geht. Dies ist besonders wichtig in Anbetracht der täglichen Mailflut.
- ist weniger formell in der Anrede („Dear John" anstatt „Dear Mr Prior, „Kind regards" anstatt „Yours sincerely"). Im vorliegenden Fall haben die Beteiligten schon eine längere Geschäftsbeziehung.

- verwendet unkomplizierte Alltagssprache („I won't be able to make it." anstatt „I will not be able to meet you." „Come and see her." anstatt „Please meet her at our stand.") und ist dadurch für den schnellen Informationsaustausch bestens geeignet. Die Sätze sind kürzer als in einem Geschäftsbrief.
- erlaubt zusammengezogene Formen wie „Thanks, I'm, won't, I'll".
- verträgt die im Internet üblichen Abkürzungen / Akronyme wie „asap" – as soon as possible, „24 / 7" – 24 hours a day, 7 days a week, „b2b" – business to business.
- hat eine Bcc-Option („Blind Carbon Copy"), also Blindkopie-Verteiler. Bitte nur spärlich verwenden, allenfalls bei Vorgängen, bei denen z. B. der Vorgesetzte vertraulich auf dem Laufenden gehalten werden soll, ansonsten lieber auf die Cc-Funktion zurückgreifen. Interessante Wortneuschöpfung: „to cc someone", jemanden auf Kopie setzen.

4.6 Was sonst noch wichtig ist

- Eine E-Mail ist ein Geschäftsdokument und sollte möglichst fehlerfrei verschickt werden. Daher: Einmal zur Kontrolle durchlesen, bevor Sie auf den Senden-Knopf klicken.
- Antworten Sie nicht sofort auf E-Mails, die Sie möglicherweise provozieren. Sie haben 24 Stunden Zeit für Ihre Antwort. Deeskalieren Sie, indem Sie mit zeitlichem Abstand sachlich reagieren. Im Zweifel einen Kollegen oder eine Kollegin zu Rate ziehen!
- Wenn Sie merken, dass Ihr Partner formeller reagiert als erwartet, stellen Sie sich bei Ihrer Antwort darauf ein.

4.7 Übungen

Exercise 1

About Business Correspondence. Work on the tasks below.

1. You're writing to a female business partner for the first time. Which of the two titles should you use, and why? *Dear Ms Miller* OR *Dear Mrs Miller.*

   Answer: Dear ______________________ is best because

   ____.

2. Correct the order (British format): a. letter head – b. reference initials – c. receiver's address – d. date – e. subject line – f. salutation
   The correct order is ____ ____ ____ ____ ____ ____.
3. Forms like "I'll, I'm, I won't" are used in ________________,

   not in __________________________.
4. True or false: British business people address their partners formally (Mr / Mrs / Ms) even after they have done business with each other for some time. ________________
5. In e-mails you can use the bcc function if you

   ____.

Exercise 2

Some E-Mail Practice

You collaborate with a software developer in the Czech Republic. Write an e-mail to your contact (Maria Czaia) there and tell her that you have put together all the missing data and that you will upload everything later today. As this happens with a delay of one week, you would like to find out whether this will postpone the completion of the software, or whether they can compensate for the extra week at their end. Also, apologize for the delay appropriately. You have had a business relationship with your partner for some time.

Exercise 3

Types of Business Documents. Match each document type on the left with a definition on the right.

1. an enquiry	a. a request to supply goods or provide services
2. a quotation	b. a letter / an e-mail to a customer about an unpaid invoice
3. an order	c. the price set (by the supplier) for goods or services
4. an invoice	d. a letter / an e-mail saying that you are not satisfied with what you received
5. a reminder	e. a request for information about a product / a service
6. a complaint	f. a bill for delivered goods or services rendered

The correct matching is: 1 ___, 2 ___, 3 ___, 4 ___, 5 ___, 6 ___.

5 Graphen beschreiben [Discussing Graphs]

5.1 Beispielabbildung und -beschreibung

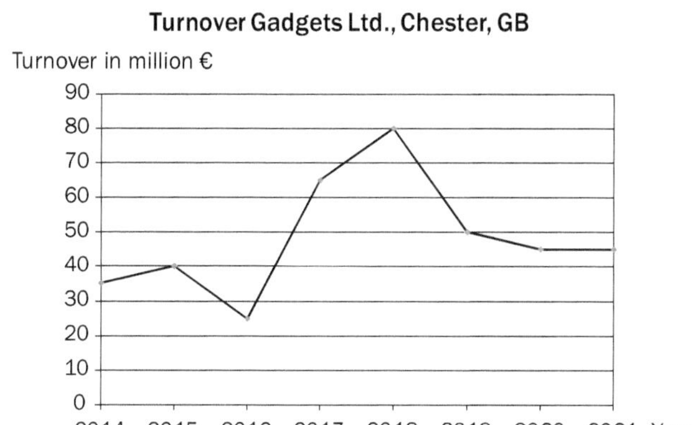

"I'd like to refer you to the first graph. It's a line graph which shows you the turnover of Gadgets Ltd between 2014 and 2021 in euros.

In 2014 the company generated a turnover of 35 million euros. Then the company extended their product range and sales increased slightly, reaching 40 million euros in 2015. In 2016, however, turnover fell steadily and bottomed out at 25 million euros. The situation improved considerably the following year when Gadgets Ltd launched a new product. Because of this, sales soared and reached 65 million euros. In 2018 turnover peaked at 80 million euros. In 2019 competition became extremely strong. As a consequence, sales had a sudden fall that year and reached only 50 million euros. The following year, due to the pandemic, turnover decreased further to 45 million euros and stayed the same in 2021."

5.2 Wortschatz

eine Aufwärtsbewegung beschreiben	to increase / go up / rise / grow / climb slightly / gently / gradually / rapidly / significantly / suddenly / sharply / dramatically to soar / rocket (*emporschnellen*) to recover (*sich erholen*) There was a significant / marked / pronounced increase. to peak / to reach a / the peak (*einen / den Höhepunkt erreichen*)
eine Abwärtsbewegung beschreiben	to decrease / go down / fall / drop / decline slightly / gently / gradually / rapidly / significantly / suddenly / sharply / dramatically There was a significant / marked / pronounced / dramatic decrease / fall / drop / downturn. to bottom out / to reach a low point / the lowest point (*einen / den Tiefpunkt erreichen*)
eine Auf- und Abwärtsbewegung beschreiben	to go up and down / fluctuate
einen gleichbleibenden Trend beschreiben	to stay the same / to stabilize / to level off
Gründe / Konsequenzen angeben	because of this / due to this / as a result / consequence
Kreisdiagramme (pie charts) beschreiben, z. B. welchen Anteil am Umsatz welches Produkt ausmacht	Smart phones represent 55 % of sales. Fitness trackers account for 20 % of sales. Tablet PCs make up 25 % of sales.

5.3 Tipps

Beachten Sie bei der Beschreibung von Diagrammen einige Grundregeln:

- Beschreiben Sie immer die Vorgänge / Entwicklungen, die sich hinter dem Diagramm verbergen, und nicht den Linienverlauf als solchen. Formulieren Sie also „As you can see, **sales** are growing steadily this year."
- Bei der Beschreibung von Vorgängen können Sie die Vergangenheitsform (Simple Past, Past Continuous Form) oder die Gegenwartsform (Simple Present, Present Continuous Form) gebrauchen. Sie können also z. B. sagen: „As you can see, profits were declining in 2018." Oder aber: „Look at this: Profits are declining in 2018 but there is a slight increase at the beginning of 2019." Sie sollten aber die Zeitformen möglichst nicht wechseln, sondern die einmal gewählte durchgängig nutzen.
- Variieren Sie Ihre Beschreibung, indem Sie zwischen den Konstruktionen Verb plus Adverb („Sales dropped dramatically.") und Adjektiv plus Substantiv („There was a sudden drop in sales.") wechseln. Formulieren Sie ruhig hin und wieder dramatisch („Sales rocketed in the first quarter.") Das wirkt nicht so eintönig und hält den Zuhörer bei der Stange.

5.4 Übungen

Exercise 1

Which part of the graph do the following verbs refer to?

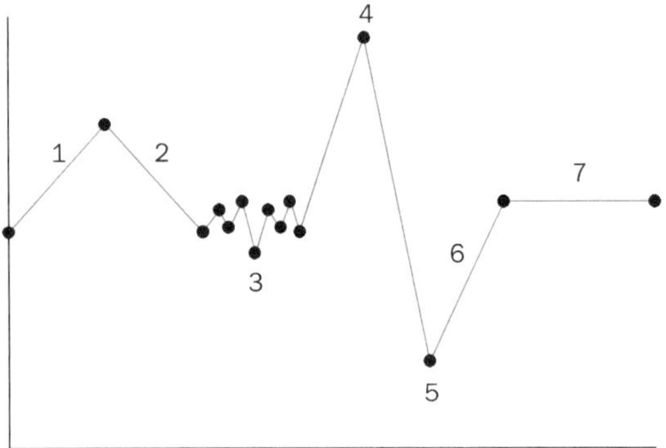

rise ____ level off ____ fluctuate ____ peak ____ recover ____
bottom out ____ fall ____

Exercise 2

Find the verbs for the following parts of the graph. Where possible, do not use the same phrases as in exercise 1.

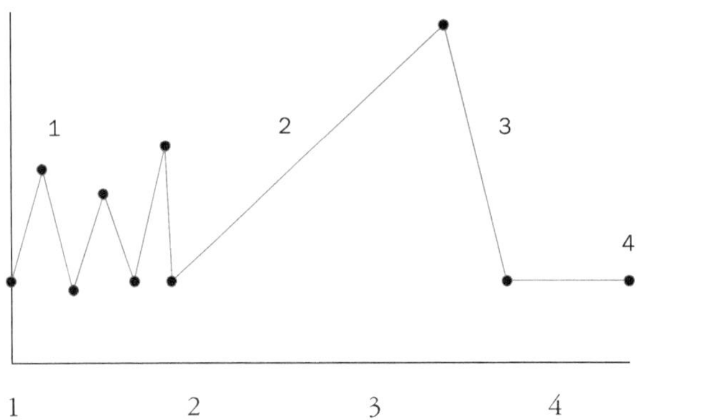

1 __________ 2 __________ 3 __________ 4 __________

Exercise 3

Graph Language: Sales Development

Describe the development of sales as shown in the graph below, using the appropriate graph language. You should write down five statements. **(XXX=Add suitable phrases.)** Do not use the same term twice. Use verb / adverb and adjective / noun phrases.

Sales:

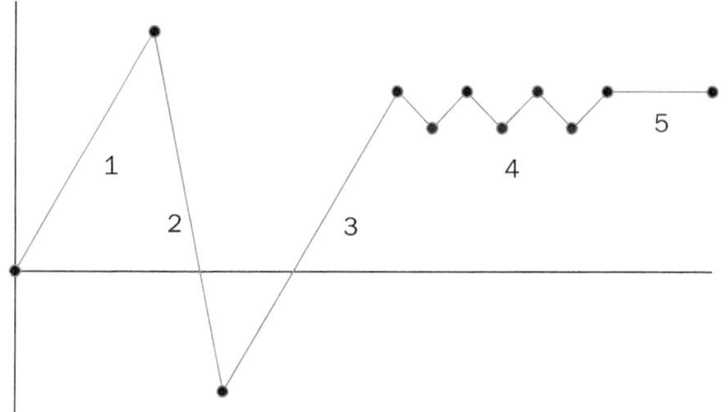

1. At first,

____

2. Then

____

3. In the following period,

____

4. XXX

____

5. XXX

____

5

Exercise 4

A Pie Chart

This pie chart shows the sales of electronic goods over a year. Discuss the diagram by making three statements about how sales are spread.

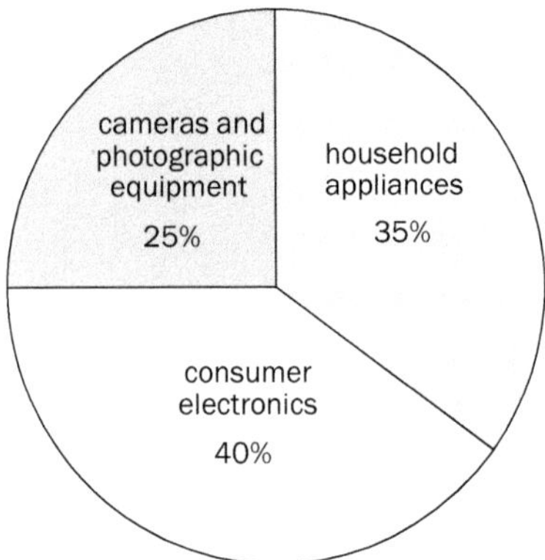

1. Household appliances

   ____.

2. Consumer electronics

   ____.

3. Cameras and electronic equipment

   ____.

6 Auf Englisch verhandeln [Negotiating in English]

6.1 Beispielverhandlung

B = Buyer, S = Supplier

B OK, shall we get down to business? I suggest today we talk about price and terms of payment for smartphones. Is this OK with you?

S I think we should add delivery terms to the agenda. (...)

B Do you think you can consider a lower price if we commit to ordering 15,000 units in the first year?

S We would be able to grant you an even bigger discount if you ordered 20,000 units to start with and 25,000 units in the years to follow. (...)

B I think the initial contract should cover two years.

S If you look at it from my point of view I'm sure you will agree that four years are much better. After all, we will be producing the phones exactly to your specifications.

B I'm willing to meet you halfway on this. Could we agree to three years?

S That's a fair proposal. (...)

B It seems that we have reached agreement on discounts, doesn't it?

S Yes, we've covered that. (...)

B Let's move on to the next item on our agenda, the delivery period. We need the smartphones urgently, as there is a strong demand for this type of product. Will you be able to deliver within three months?

S I'm afraid this might be a bit too tight. We are willing to make a part delivery, say 5,000 units, three months after receipt of order. The remaining items will be delivered one month later. How does this sound?

B OK, but 5,000 within three months is a must. (...)

S OK. Can we review what we have agreed on so far?

B Yes, that would be useful.

6.2 Wortschatz

die Verhandlung beginnen	Shall we get down to business? Let's get down to business. Shall we make a start? Let's get started.
die Tagesordnung festlegen	Let's agree on the agenda first. I suggest we talk about … first and then move on to … Can we add an item to the agenda? There are … items on the agenda. Shall we take the points in this order?
von einem Punkt zum anderen gehen	So, let's start with … Why don't we start with …? Let's move on to the next item on our agenda, which is … Now that we've agreed on … let's turn to the next item on the agenda.
einen Vorschlag machen	Do you think you can consider a lower price / a higher discount if we commit to …? Would it be possible for you to …? May I propose that … How about …? Why don't we / you …?
einen Gegenvorschlag machen	If you look at it from my point of view, I'm sure you will agree that … How about …instead? Could you consider …instead? Would you find … acceptable? I'm not too happy with that. What about … instead? May I suggest an alternative?

Kompromisse finden	I'm willing to meet you halfway on this. Shall we split the difference and say three years? Could we agree to three years? – That's a fair proposal. In return for this, would you be willing to …? We would be ready to accept this; however there would be one condition. …
auf einem Punkt bestehen	It is crucial / essential for us to … This is a must. I'm sorry, we can't accept this. We will not be able to reach a reasonable profit margin (*Gewinnspanne*). That's totally unacceptable.
dem Ergebnis zustimmen	It seems that we have reached agreement on … I think we have an agreement. It's a deal!
die Ergebnisse zusammenfassen	Let's quickly go over today's main points. Can we review what we have agreed on so far? Let's recap on our main points. Let's summarize what we've agreed on today. Yes, a summary would be useful.

6.3 Tipps

Verhandeln auf Englisch ist komplex; Sie sprechen in der Fremdsprache, Ihr Gegenüber möglicherweise in seiner Muttersprache. Diesen Wettbewerbsnachteil sollten Sie durch eine gute Vorbereitung ausgleichen, insbesondere in sprachlicher Hinsicht.

- Formulieren Sie stets höflich unter Verwendung von modalen Hilfsverben: „May I suggest / propose ...? Could we ...? Would you agree that ...? Shall we ...?“ Dies ist wichtig für eine entspannte Atmosphäre und einen respektvollen Umgang miteinander.
- Wenn Sie nicht nur vereinzelt, sondern berufsbedingt häufig verhandeln müssen, lohnt sich eine grammatische Trainingseinheit: Wiederholen Sie die „If-Sätze“ (Typ I und II). Beim Verhandeln kommen diese häufig zum Einsatz, z. B. in Formulierungen wie „If you look at it from my point of view you will agree that ...“ (Typ I, erfüllbare Bedingung) oder „If you agreed to this, we would be able to move a step in your direction.“ (Typ II, Möglichkeit)
- Stellen Sie zwischendurch immer wieder sicher, dass Sie alles richtig verstanden haben („If I understand you correctly, ... / May I summarize what we have just said?“). Fassen Sie nach dem Treffen alle Ergebnisse schriftlich, z. B. in einer E-Mail, zusammen, damit beide Seiten letzte Missverständnisse ausräumen können.

6.4 Übungen

Exercise 1

Complete the following statements. They all deal with negotiation language.

1. You should have received the ____________________ for today's meeting. Are there any additional points you'd like to cover?
2. There is no time to lose. Let's ____________________ business.
3. The initial ____________________ is for three years.
4. Shall we split the ____________________ and say one and a half?
5. I have to insist on a wholesale price of 230 euros. This figure will give us a reasonable ____________________ margin.
6. What are your terms of ____________________?

7. O.K then. Aluminium legs and frame, metal top 100 x 160 cm. It's good we have covered the ________________.
8. Now, what have we agreed on? A quick ________________ will be useful.

Exercise 2

You have just negotiated an agreement with a business partner. Please write an e-mail to him / her and summarize the following results:

Product: metal garden chair
- weight: 11.6 kg
- made of 22 mm steel tube (=*Stahlrohr*)
- black

Wholesale price: 75 €
Chairs to be supplied year 1: 15,000
Chairs to be supplied year 2: 20,000, then new quantities to be negotiated
Duration of Agreement: 3 years
Delivery to begin: 4 months from now to make sure that chairs arrive before the summer season.

Don't forget to thank your partner for the meeting and say that you are looking forward very much to working with him / her.

Dear David / Dear Josephine

It was good to …

Kind regards
XXX

Exercise 3

The following phrases (left) are from negotiation language. Match them to their definitions or synonyms on the right.

1. summary	a. length of time
2. reach agreement	b. an offer
3. agenda items	c. sending goods to the customer
4. terms	d. say clearly what you want
5. a proposal	e. conditions
6. duration	f. listing the results of your discussion
7. delivery	g. find a solution which suits both sides
8. state a position	h. subjects

The correct order is 1 ___, 2 ___, 3 ___, 4 ___, 5 ___, 6 ___, 7 ___, 8 ___.

7 Auf Englisch präsentieren [Presenting in English]

7.1 Beispielpräsentation

"Good afternoon, ladies and gentlemen. My name's Stephanie Clark. I'm the marketing & sales director of SEON, a start-up company that offers online services to learners of English. Now, you may wonder what SEON means. Actually, it's an acronym which stands for "Study English Online".
I'd like to talk to you today about our innovative service for language students which is available in Germany and some other European countries. I'll be addressing three main points in my presentation. First, I'm going to give you a general overview of what our website has to offer in order to facilitate the learning process. In my second point I'd like to look in more detail at the advantages of studying a language online, with a special focus on vocabulary and grammar, using lots of examples from our website. And finally, in my third point, I'll be showing you how you, as teachers, can benefit from our services in your own classroom. This presentation will take about 45 minutes. If you have any questions, I'll be glad to answer them after I have finished my talk.
OK, to start with, I'd like you to take a look at our website. As you can see (...)
In the first part of my presentation I've outlined what our website can offer to your students. Let's now move on to my second point. I'd like to invite you to actually do some vocab and grammar exercises online, which will help you to evaluate what benefits there are for the students. (...)
That's all I have to say about the different types of online activities. The third and final point I'd like to discuss is how you can make your teaching even more attractive by taking advantage of our online services. We've developed a special feature for that

purpose which I'd like to demonstrate to you. As I've already said, (...)
Let me just summarize my main points. Today we've looked at ...
I've now come to the end of my talk. I hope I've been able to make you familiar with our innovative learning and teaching services. If you have any questions, I'll be glad to answer them right now. Thank you very much for your attention."

7.2 Wortschatz

das Publikum begrüßen und sich vorstellen	Good morning / afternoon / evening, ladies and gentlemen / colleagues / fellow students. My name is ... I'm the marketing director / CEO / ... of ...
das Thema einführen und auf Frage-möglichkeiten hinweisen	I'd like to say a few words today about ... / talk to you today about ... / explain to you today the ... In my presentation I'm going to explain ... I've divided my talk into ... main parts. I'll be addressing ... main points in my presentation. This presentation / talk will take about ... minutes. If you have any questions, I'll be glad to answer them after I have finished my talk. I'll be happy to take your questions after my talk. If you have any questions, please feel free to interrupt me at any time.
den ersten Punkt einführen	To start with, I'd like to consider ... First of all, I'd like to look at ... OK, let's get going. The first point I'd like to make / discuss is ...

einen Punkt abschließen	That's all I have to say about … Now we've looked at / dealt with / discussed …
von einem Punkt zum anderen wechseln – Beziehungen zwischen den Argumenten herstellen	Now let's turn to … / move on to … The next point I'd like to make is … Secondly … / Thirdly… I'd like to talk about … However / on the other hand / although / in spite of this …(*Gegensätze ausdrücken*) Therefore / so / consequently / because of this / as a result …(*kausale Zusammenhänge darstellen*) Furthermore … / Moreover… / In addition to this… / Finally…(*Punkte aneinanderreihen*)
sich auf bereits Gesagtes beziehen / ausdrücken, dass etwas später behandelt wird / auf Fragen reagieren	As I said at the beginning … As I've already said, … As I mentioned earlier, … I'll come to that later. I'll return to this point in a few minutes. If you don't mind, I'll answer this question at the end of my presentation. Can we get back to this a bit later?
die Präsentation zusammenfassen	So now I'd just like to summarize the main points. If I may just recap the most important points.
Schlüsse ziehen und sich verabschieden	That's all I have to say for now. I think that covers most of the points. That concludes my talk. OK, that brings me to the end of the presentation. I'd like to thank you for … Thank you for your attention.

zu Fragen einladen	And now, if you have any questions, I'll be glad to answer them. I would welcome any comments / suggestions. OK, we only have a few minutes left. Is there one last question?

7.3 Tipps

Was sollten Sie bei einer Präsentation (nicht nur) in der Fremdsprache beachten? Eine gründliche Vorbereitung ist entscheidend. Dazu zählt zunächst einmal, dass Sie Ihr Thema zu 100 % beherrschen. Aber nicht nur das:

- Überlegen Sie, welche Ziele Sie mit Ihrer Präsentation verfolgen (Verkauf, Training, Information etc.). Danach richten sich Inhalt und Aufbau Ihres Vortrags. Wenn Sie sich selbst nicht genau darüber im Klaren sind, können Sie auch Ihr Publikum nicht überzeugen.
- Reisen Sie deutlich vor Beginn der Veranstaltung an, um den Raum kennenzulernen. Das gibt Selbstvertrauen.
- Planen Sie die Länge Ihrer Präsentation genau nach Vorgabe, überziehen Sie nicht. Ihr Publikum wird es Ihnen danken.
- Strukturieren Sie Ihre Präsentation gemäß der Tabelle oben.
- Nehmen Sie Ihr Publikum mit auf Ihre gedankliche Reise. Benutzen Sie „signpost language" (siehe Tabelle oben), die den Zuhörer jederzeit darüber informiert, wo Sie sich gerade befinden („The second point I'd like to discuss…"). Eine Übersicht zu Beginn und eine Zusammenfassung am Ende sind zwingend!
- Unterstützen Sie Ihre Präsentation visuell (PowerPoint, Flipchart). Bedenken Sie: Nur 20 % der Informationen werden über das Hören aufgenommen, 80 % durch visuelle Wahrnehmung. Folien oder Charts bieten noch einen weiteren Vorteil: Sie können Ihre Schlüsselaussagen auf Englisch perfekt vorbereiten und sich während des Vortrags darauf beziehen. Das gibt Ihnen die nötige Selbstsicherheit!

- Lesen Sie Ihre Folien nicht vor, erläutern Sie die Kernaussagen, dem Publikum zugewandt (Blickkontakt!). Nutzen Sie Karteikarten, auf die Sie während des Vortrags zurückgreifen können.
- Spielen Sie Ihre Präsentation zwei- bis dreimal durch, vor Freunden oder im Zweifel vor dem Spiegel. Das hilft Ihnen, die (Fach) Sprache zu trainieren und den Zeitbedarf zu überprüfen und ggf. anzupassen. So wird's gelingen!

7.4 Übungen

Exercise 1

Check the following phrases from a presentation about a new smart gadget and put them in the right order.

1. Let's now move on to environmental aspects. Recycling the gadget is no problem. Mechanical and plastic parts as well as the battery can be separated easily.
2. Finally, I'd like to draw your attention to some major privacy issues.
3. Today I'm going to talk about a new tech gadget that will help you to make your home smart.
4. And now, if you have any questions, I'll be glad to answer them.
5. To sum up, the new gadget will make your life much easier in many respects, but it comes at a price. Data protection is still a problem.
6. First of all, I'd like to talk about the technical specifications.

The correct order is ___, ___, ___, ___, ___, ___.

Exercise 2

Signposting language. Write the phrases from the box for each part of your presentation in the correct group.

Now let's move on to … • If I may recap the most important points. • Good morning, colleagues. • However, … • I've divided my talk into three main parts. • As I've already mentioned … • My name is … • Let me summarize the main points. • On the other hand, … • The next point I'd like to make is … • In my presentation I'm going to explain … • Can we get back to this a bit later?

Greeting the audience/ Introducing yourself	Introducing the topic	Moving from one point to the next	Referring to something said before/ dealing with questions	Introducing contrasting arguments	Summarizing the results of your presentation

Exercise 3

Are the following statements about presentations true or false?

1. About 80 % of information is absorbed through words and sounds and about 20 % visually.
2. Slides (*Folien*) are useful because you can read out everything to your audience.
3. It is essential to rehearse your presentation before you actually deliver it.
4. Signposting language and visuals will help your audience to process information more effectively.
5. You should arrive at the presentation venue together with your audience.

8 Ein Meeting leiten [Chairing a Meeting]

8.1 Beispielsituation

Chair (Lisa) Good afternoon everyone, can I have your attention please?
Thank you all for coming to today's meeting. Perhaps we can make a start now. Would you please take the minutes, Ben? Thank you.
The objective of our meeting is to prepare the launch of David Hilby's new novel, which is to appear in three months. We'll go over the online marketing campaign and talk about how to approach the key bookshops. We'll also discuss how we can involve David, who's more than happy to assist us with the campaign. I'm glad that Mila from our marketing agency has joined us here today, and also Michael, David's agent.
The first item on the agenda is how our online campaign can produce best results. For this, we need to define our target markets, select the channels we want to use, and discuss the role of social networks.
...
Would anyone like to add their ideas? Yes, Sophia?

Sophia Shouldn't we also discuss search engine optimization in order to get higher rankings?

Chair I see your point, Sophia, this is an important issue. However, we have a tight schedule today. Let's table it for the next meeting.
If no one has anything else to add, we can move on to the second item, which is how to approach the major bookshops in the country. Mila, would you like to talk about the agency's ideas here?

Mila Certainly. Thank you for inviting me today. I'd like to start by discussing the role of the field reps. They ...

Chair	Thank you, Mila. It's good to know that the agency has developed an innovative concept. I think this covers the second item of our agenda. I'd like to hand over to Michael, who will be illustrating how David Hilby can boost the campaign. Michael, the floor is yours.
Michael	Thank you, Lisa. Well, first of all, David sends his greetings to all of you. …
Chair	Thank you, Michael. I think this is all we can say about David's role at the moment. Yes, Ben, I see you'd like to make a final comment on this matter?
Ben	Yes, I wonder whether David could come to the publishing house and meet the staff here. That would increase motivation considerably.
Chair	Ben, let's not get too far off-topic here. This is something we can come back to once everything else has been wrapped up. O. K. It looks like we've covered the main items of the meeting today. To sum up, we discussed online marketing for the new book and listed the steps to be taken next. Then Mila introduced us to the campaign the agency has prepared for our key customers, the bookshops. And, finally, we agreed that David Hilby will be starting a reading tour immediately after publication. Is there any other business? If not, I'd like to thank you all for attending the meeting. The follow-up meeting will take place exactly in two weeks. Goodbye for now.

8.2 Wortschatz

die Teilnehmer begrüßen	Good afternoon everyone, can I have your attention please? Good to see you all here today. I'd like to welcome you all here today. Thank you all for coming (at such short notice). We're pleased to welcome …
das Meeting beginnen	Can we make a start? Has everyone got a copy of the agenda? Shall we get down to business? Let's begin. Let's get the ball rolling. Without further ado I'd like to open the discussion. Could someone take the minutes please? Would you please take the minutes, …?
in das Thema einführen	The aim / objective of our meeting is to … Today's meeting is about … I've called this meeting to discuss … There are three items on our agenda. First, …
einen Punkt beenden, einen neuen beginnen	I think that covers the first item. I think that takes care of the second item. Well, it seems that we're done with the first item. If nobody has anything else to add, … Let's move on to the next item on the agenda. Why don't we move on to … Now we come to …

das Meeting managen, Teilnehmer einbeziehen, auf die Zeit achten	Would anyone like to add their ideas? What's your position on that, …? I would appreciate your input on this. I think we need to put forward a motion. Can we put this to the vote? The floor is yours. Over to you. Let's table this for / shelve this until the next meeting. Let's wrap this up first. Let's not get too far off-topic here. Let's not get off the subject. Can we get back to the agenda? Could we keep the discussion to the point? I'm afraid we're running out of time.
die Ergebnisse zusammenfassen	Before we close, let me summarize the main points. To sum up, … / to recap, … Briefly, the main points we have discussed are …
das Meeting beenden	Is there any other business? Are there any questions before we finish? Well, if there are no further comments, let's call it a day. I think this just about covers everything. Right, that's all for today's meeting. I guess that's all for today.
die Teilnehmer verabschieden	Thank you all for coming. That was a fruitful discussion. Thank you for attending. Thanks for your participation. See you in two weeks.

8.3 Tipps

- Der/die Vorsitzende eines Meetings wird „chairperson" oder meistens einfach nur „chair" genannt. Das entsprechende Verb heißt „to chair a meeting".
- Aufgepasst bei „minutes" in diesem Zusammenhang: Das Wort hat hier nichts mit Zeit zu tun, sondern mit dem Protokoll der Sitzung: „Can you take the minutes please?"
- „Let's table/shelve it until the next meeting." Die zwei Verben drücken aus, dass Sie Punkte auf die nächste Sitzung verschieben möchten.
- Sie übergeben das Wort an jemanden mit den folgenden Wendungen: „The floor is yours." Oder: „Over to you."
- In formellen Sitzungen kommt es manchmal zu einer Abstimmung eines Antrags („motion"): „Can we put this to the vote? All those in favour? All those against? OK, we have 8 votes for and 3 votes against. So that's agreed."
- Wenn Sie sich fragen, was „AOB" auf der Tagesordnung bedeutet: Die Abkürzung für „Any Other Business" entspricht dem deutschen TOP „Verschiedenes" oder „Sonstiges".
- „Let's call it a day.": eine lockere Redewendung, um eine Sitzung zu beenden.

8.4 Übungen

Exercise 1

Find the correct words/phrases.

1. A list of items to be discussed at a meeting is called

   ____
2. written record of a meeting ______________________
3. purpose of a meeting ______________________
4. coming to a meeting ______________________ a meeting
5. the person who runs a meeting ______________________

6. over to you ______________________

7. not relevant to the current discussion ______________________

8. AOB stands for ______________________

Exercise 2

Put the following phrases in the right order.

1 Let me recap • 2 Let's get the ball rolling. • 3 Good to see you all here today. • 4 The aim of our meeting is … • 5 I guess that's all for today. • 6 Can I have your attention please?

The correct order is __, __, __, __, __, __.

Exercise 3

The following scrambled words are all from Unit 8. Can you identify the originals?

1. TIANEONTT ______________________
2. OUSEPRP ______________________
3. AIMPNCGA ______________________
4. MEIT ______________________
5. DEUHLCSE ______________________
6. EOMMNCT ______________________
7. RPWA PU ______________________
8. CPARE ______________________
9. RSZMEMUAI ______________________
10. VEORC ______________________

9 Sich auf Englisch bewerben [Applying for a Position in English]

9.1 Modell-CV (internationaler Standard)

Konrad Berger ①

Contact Details	Mobile: +49 176 20 678 207 E-Mail: k.berger@capital.de ② linkedin.com/in/konrad-berger-77664433a	
Career Objective	Entry-level Position in Sales/Customer Service ③	
Summary	▪ Expertise in operating CRM systems such as SAP Sales Cloud ④ ▪ Customer-oriented approach to work ▪ Experienced in handling pressure/challenging customers ▪ Ability to collaborate effectively with the Sales Team ▪ Bachelor's degree in Business Administration specializing in the Digital Economy	
Work Experience ⑤		
eBay, Kleinmachnow, Berlin	Internship semester in Customer Service ▪ tracked/analyzed customer website activities ▪ investigated failed products related to the eBay platforms and offered solutions or recommendations ▪ liaised closely with the Sales Team to reach sales targets ⑥ ▪ contributed to Knowledge Base/FAQ and other customer-facing support resources	3/2019 - 9/2019
Quietcorner.de, Berlin (restaurant reservation platform)	Internship in Contract Management ▪ administered contract data in a content management system ▪ optimized customer booking processes ▪ responded to customer queries via social media ▪ updated the customer database	8/2018 - 10/2018 8/2017 - 10/2017

Gap Year in Australia	Work and Travel ■ guided tours at beach-resort sight-seeing attractions ■ served customers at a tourist shop ■ worked as a waiter in a hotel restaurant	10/2015 – 9/2016	
Education			⑦
Technische Hochschule Berlin (University of Applied Sciences)	BSc in Business Administration – Specialization in the Digital Economy	10/2016 – 3/2020	
Lise-Meitner-Gymnasium, Dresden	*Abitur* (university entrance certificate / A-Levels)	9/2007 – 7/2015	
Special Skills / Interests			⑧
Microsoft programs	Office, Project, Access		
Further computer programs	SAP ERP, Drupal, Typo3		
Languages	German (native speaker), English (C1), Spanish (A2)		
Hobbies	Volleyball, football referee		⑨

9.2 Wortschatz

Describing professional activities / achievements	
to supervise a team	ein Team leiten
to acquire XX new customers within one year	in einem Jahr XX neue Kunden akquirieren
to consult with / visit key customers regularly	Schlüsselkunden regelmäßig besuchen
to plan and realize projects	Projekte planen und koordinieren
to expand the product portfolio	das Produktportfolio erweitern

to develop / introduce a new product / service	ein neues Produkt / ein neues Dienstleistungsangebot entwickeln / einführen
to plan the launch of XX	die Markteinführung des Produkts XX planen
to increase sales / the market share of XX by XX % over XX years	Umsätze / den Marktanteil von XX innerhalb von XX Jahren um XX % steigern
to achieve XX % savings in the cost range of XX	XX % Kosteneinsparungen im Bereich XX realisieren
to write quarterly reports on XX	Quartalsberichte über XX schreiben
to initiate measures for XX / XX (ing-form)	Maßnahmen für etwas einleiten
Action verbs for applicants with little work experience	
to support the marketing / sales manager	den Marketingleiter / die Verkaufsleiterin unterstützen
to be in a team that successfully introduced XX / contributed considerably to the successful introduction of XX	Mitglied eines Teams sein, das erfolgreich XX eingeführt hat / das einen wesentlichen Beitrag zur Einführung von XX geleistet hat
to assist the line manager with XX / in XX (ing-form)	dem Vorgesetzten / der Vorgesetzten bei XX assistieren

9.3 Tipps CV

Der Lebenslauf ist das Kernstück einer jeden Bewerbung. Im britischen Englisch bezeichnet man ihn als „CV“ (curriculum vitae), im Amerikanischen als „résumé / resume“. Beide Dokumente unterscheiden sich in einigen Punkten von dem in deutschsprachigen Ländern üblichen Lebenslauf, wobei auch bei uns eine Entwicklung zu einem internationalen Standard erkennbar ist, der hier als Modell dient.

Und das ist für Sie wichtig (entlang des Modell-CVs):

① Schreiben Sie Ihren vollen Namen als Überschrift (typographisch hervorgehoben) über Ihren CV. Es geht um Sie, Sie stehen im Mittelpunkt, Sie betreiben Marketing in eigener Sache. Keine falsche Bescheidenheit!

② Ihre Kontaktdetails finden sich ganz oben im CV. Wenn Sie beruflich in sozialen Netzwerken unterwegs sind (z. B. *LinkedIn*, *XING*), fügen Sie den Pfad zu Ihrem Profil hinzu. **Ganz wichtig**: In englischsprachigen Ländern ist ein Foto unüblich, in Nordamerika führt das Einfügen eines Fotos u. U. sogar zur Ablehnung der Bewerbung (US-amerikanische Gesetzgebung gegen Diskriminierung). Aus demselben Grund sollten Sie bei Bewerbungen **im englischsprachigen Bereich** auf Hinweise auf Alter, Gender, Religion, Herkunft, Familienstand / Kinder, Gesundheit unbedingt verzichten.

③ Fahren Sie von Anfang eine klare Linie: Was ist Ihr nächstes Karriereziel, worauf bewerben Sie sich (**Career Objective**)? Bei einer Initiativbewerbung fassen Sie dieses Karriereziel nicht zu eng: Nennen Sie lieber ein Arbeitsgebiet wie oben.

④ Denken Sie daran: Der Leser / die Leserin Ihrer Bewerbung steht in der Regel unter Zeitdruck. Machen Sie es ihm / ihr sehr einfach, Ihre Vorzüge zu erkennen. Das Wichtigste auf einen Blick (**Summary**) ist ein geeignetes Hilfsmittel dazu: kurz, „knackig", informativ, d. h. Qualifikationen, die sich genau auf diese Stelle beziehen, also nicht allgemeingültige Qualifikationen wie z. B. Englischkenntnisse oder Beherrschen von Microsoft-Programmen.

⑤ Der gesamte CV ist in umgekehrter chronologischer Reihenfolge organisiert. Denn im Allgemeinen sind die jüngsten Arbeitserfahrungen für den Arbeitgeber relevanter als die älteren oder die Ausbildung. Beginnen Sie also in der Regel mit der **Work Experience**.

⑥ Englischsprachige Bewerbungen sind dynamisch, d. h. sie spiegeln das wieder, was Sie durch konkrete Tätigkeiten erreicht haben. Deswegen werden gerne „**action verbs**" (to log, check, enter etc.) benutzt. Weitere Beispiele finden Sie oben wie unten.

⑦ Ausbildung (**Education**): Hier ebenfalls mit dem jüngsten Schritt (Abschluss des Studiums) beginnen. Alles ab Abitur zählt (kann mit zunehmender Qualifikation weggelassen werden), die Ausbildungsschritte vorher sind nicht relevant. Lassen Sie deutsche Eigenbegriffe in *kursiv* stehen (*Abitur*) und sagen Sie kurz, was sie auf Englisch bedeuten (AE: **university entrance certificate,** BE: **A-Levels**). Fachhochschulen werden immer als **University of Applied Sciences** bezeichnet.

⑧ Bei **Special Skills / Interests** ergänzen Sie wesentliche Fertigkeiten und Qualifikationen, die für die ausgeschriebene Position relevant sind. Ihre Sprachkenntnisse ordnen Sie möglichst gemäß dem Europäischen Referenzrahmen ein (https://www.europaeischer-referenzrahmen.de/). Damit können Personaler etwas anfangen.

⑨ Auch **Hobbys** [aufgepasst! – auf Englisch **Hobbies**], die Sie betreiben, können positive Hinweise auf Ihre Einstellungen und Fähigkeiten sowie Persönlichkeit liefern. Sind Sie etwa Schiedsrichter (**referee**), dann sind Sie gewohnt, mit Konfliktsituationen umzugehen und Entscheidungen zu treffen. Ballsport weist auf Teamfähigkeit hin, längere Reisen in ferne Länder auf Offenheit und Neugier sowie Problemlösungskompetenz.

Ein amerikanisches „résumé" wird in der Regel nicht mit Datum und Unterschrift versehen, bei einem britischen CV ist dies auch nicht zwingend notwendig, aber möglich.

9.4 Modell Covering Letter / Cover Letter

Konrad Berger
Luxemburger Str. 10
13353 Berlin, Germany
k.berger@capital.de
+49 176 20 678 207

15 November 20XX

Ms Julie Snowdon
SmartyDigy Ltd.
HR Department ①
3rd Floor
Albion House
Hammersmith Rd
London W5 9MH
UK

Dear Ms Snowdon ②

Application for an entry-level position in Sales / Customer Service ③

Your company has been recommended to me by Alena Watford, who is currently working in your Accounts Department. She believes that you are interested in employing someone with experience in customer service. ④

I have recently graduated from the Technische Hochschule Berlin (University of Applied Sciences) with a Bachelor's degree in Business Administration specializing in the Digital Economy. I am looking for an entry-level position in e-Commerce with an innovative tech company like SmartyDigy Ltd.

My area of specialization concerns the improvement of measures regarding customer service. I have acquired extensive experience in this field as listed below:

- troubleshooting failed products related to sales platforms and offering solutions or recommendations
- optimizing administration processes in contract management by simplifying the entry of personal data ⑤
- reducing customer response time by using messaging and social networks when answering queries

My enclosed CV provides information regarding further duties I performed in the digital economy during my internships.

I would be very pleased to meet you personally or virtually to explain how I can contribute to SmartyDigy's success. I will be available from January of next year.

If you would like any additional information, please let me know. Thank you for your interest in my application. I look forward to hearing from you soon. ⑥

Yours sincerely

Konrad Berger

Encl. CV

9.5 Wortschatz

application for	Bewerbung auf (eine Position)
to apply for	sich bewerben auf
to apply to a company	sich bei einer Firma bewerben
job / position	eine Stelle / Position [aufgepasst! – im Englischen hat *job* wenig Stellenwert]
to recommend s. o. to	jmd. empfehlen, eine Empfehlung aussprechen für
to employ s. o.	jmd. anstellen
experience in	Erfahrungen im Bereich

to graduate from XX University	einen akademischen Abschluss an der Hochschule / Universität XX machen
to specialize in	einen Schwerpunkt auf etwas legen
entry-level position	Einstiegsposition
area of specialization	Spezialisierungsgebiete
to acquire / gain / gather experience	Erfahrungen sammeln [not *collect*!]
hands-on / practical solutions	praktische Lösungen
to provide information	Informationen zur Verfügung stellen
to perform duties	Aufgaben erledigen
to do / serve an internship (AE), to do a work placement (BE)	ein Praktikum, auch Praxissemester, absolvieren
to contribute to	zu etwas beitragen
available	verfügbar

Best alternatives
„apply for a position / post" (*post* = höhere Positionen) klingt deutlich anspruchsvoller als „apply for a job" (einfachere Tätigkeiten). „Experience" im Singular hat im Englischen die umfassendere Bedeutung und verweist nicht nur auf isolierte Einzelerfahrungen (experiences).

9.6 Tipps zum Anschreiben

Da fehlt doch etwas zu einer erfolgreichen Bewerbung? Richtig, das Anschreiben (BE: **covering letter**, AE **cover letter**). Auch hier das Wichtigste auf einen Blick (entlang des Modells).

Generell: Das Anschreiben dient **nicht** der Zusammenfassung des CVs. Vielmehr akzentuieren und erläutern Sie das, was für die ausgeschriebene Position besonders wichtig ist. Das Dokument ist somit nicht weniger bedeutsam als der CV.

Machen Sie deutlich, dass Sie sich mit dem Produktportfolio der Firma beschäftigt haben. Schließlich wollen Sie sich selbst bald damit identifizieren.

① Das Anschreiben ist wie ein Geschäftsbrief aufgebaut und folgt dessen Regeln (vgl. Kapitel 4). Es gibt wiederum Unterschiede zwischen einem Anschreiben in Großbritannien und Nordamerika. Das hier vorgeschlagene Format ist international einsetzbar.
② Recherchieren Sie den Ansprechpartner bzw. die Ansprechpartnerin und nutzen Sie den Namen im Anschreiben, auch wenn dieser nicht in der Stellenausschreibung zu finden ist. Sie zeigen damit Interesse an Ihrem Gegenüber!
③ Sagen Sie in der Betreffzeile kurz und bündig, auf welche Position Sie sich bewerben.
④ Machen Sie deutlich, wie Sie von der Vakanz erfahren haben (hier: Empfehlung).
⑤ Arbeiten Sie auch hier mit „action verbs," oben im „covering letter" in Form von „gerunds" (ing-Verben). Welche zwei oder drei Kerntätigkeiten der letzten Arbeitsstelle oder Ihres Praktikums sind besonders wichtig für die Position, auf die Sie sich bewerben? Die höchste Wirkung erzielen Stichpunkte (in Form von „bullet points"), um mit Ihren wichtigsten Qualifikationen Interesse zu wecken.
⑥ Beenden Sie das Anschreiben freundlich und positiv. Schließlich sind Sie darauf angewiesen, dass der zukünftige Arbeitgeber Ihrer Bewerbung wohlwollend gegenübersteht.

Versuchen Sie, das Anschreiben auf ¾ Seite zu beschränken.

Ganz wichtig sind zusammenfassend die folgenden Aspekte:

Bewerberinnen und Bewerber im deutschsprachigen Kulturraum tendieren zu Bescheidenheit und Zurückhaltung in ihren Dokumenten. Das ist im angelsächsischen Bereich deutlich anders: Eine Bewerbung wird als **Marketingkampagne in eigener Sache** gesehen, der Bewerber bzw. die Bewerberin steht in Konkurrenz zu anderen. Es geht darum, sich selbstbewusst auf Erreichtes zu beziehen, klare Zielvorstellungen zu formulieren und die Dokumente ansprechend zu präsentieren. Auch junge Menschen zu Beginn ihrer Karriere haben bereits Leistungen erbracht, Ziele erreicht, Kompetenzen geschärft. Versuchen Sie, sich dieses „Mindset" zu eigen zu machen: Gesundes Selbstbewusstsein transportieren, ganz ohne Überheblichkeit, das ist gut möglich. Es ist der erste Eindruck, der zählt und der sich beim Personaler bzw. bei der Personalerin verfestigt. Tun Sie alles dafür, dass dieser positiv ist.

Lebenslauf und Anschreiben sollten daher **fehlerfrei** sein, unabhängig davon, in welcher Form sie eingereicht werden. Folgende Methoden zur Überprüfung haben sich bewährt:

- Das Rechtschreibeprogramm auf Ihrem Computer kann erste wichtige Dienste leisten, reicht aber nicht aus.
- Geben Sie die Dokumente jemandem mit sehr guten Englischkenntnissen zum Gegenlesen. Muttersprachler sind natürlich die beste Wahl.
- Fehler lassen sich auf ausgedruckten Dokumenten oft leichter identifizieren als auf dem Bildschirm.

Das Format dieses Büchleins erlaubt lediglich einen ersten Überblick über notwendige Bewerbungsdokumente; es lohnt sich für Sie, sich umfassender zu informieren, z. B. mit Hilfe der Literatur, die in der Auswahlbibliographie gelistet ist. Manche Veröffentlichungen bieten sehr hilfreiche Wortlisten, abgestimmt auf die Struktur des CVs bzw. des Anschreibens. Damit kann wenig schiefgehen!

9.7 Übungen

In the following four exercises, choose the correct words from the boxes. The vocabulary is most useful for both your CV and covering letter.

Exercise 1

Summary

team player • employed • independent • excellent skills • experience • Product Manager

1. More than 5 years ________________ in sales.
2. Presently ________________ as ________________ at Siemens AG.
3. ________________ in organisation and negotiating.
4. ________________ worker yet also effective ________________

Exercise 2

Current Employment

writing • obtaining / getting / reaching • negotiating • increasing • running / supervising • 10 % • forwarding • responsible for / in charge of • reducing

1. During my years at Siemens I have been ________________ the following areas:
2. ________________ a team of five experts.
3. ________________ contracts worth €250,000 with international customers.
4. ________________ questionnaires to potential customers.
5. ________________ quarterly reports.

6. ________________ response time significantly by using messaging and social networks.
7. ________________ sales of smart home gadgets by ________________ over two years.
8. ________________ 30 % market share for new circuit breakers within one year.

Exercise 3

Previous Employment

developed / designed • part • planned / organized / prepared • expanded

1. ________________ of a team at Bosch Rexroth where I was responsible for the following tasks:
2. ________________ the implementation of a new hydraulic system.
3. ________________ an innovative computer-controlled valve.
4. ________________ the product portfolio.

Exercise 4

Special Skills and Interests

extensive / comprehensive • C1 • request • skills • available

1. Excellent computer ________________.
2. ________________ knowledge of Microsoft Office programs.
3. Spoken and written English at ________________ level.
4. References ________________ upon ________________.

10 Falsche Freunde [False Friends]

"False Friends" are words that are often mixed up with words in another language with a different meaning.

10.1 Beispiel

The word "Homeoffice" has become very popular in the German language. Be careful, in English it is normally used with a different meaning. The term "Home Office" refers to the governmental department in Great Britain dealing with domestic matters (*Innenministerium*). If you want to say that you work for your company in your house or flat, you say that you **work from home**. "False Friends" can lead to funny, sometimes embarrassing situations.

10.2 Übungen

Check these 20 common "False Friends" by replacing the wrong words **in bold.**

1. The **actual** train timetable can be downloaded from the website.
2. The professor never seems to be able to connect his notebook with the **beamer**.
3. I'll have to talk to the **chef** about a pay rise soon.
4. The official **controlled** our passports when we passed the border.
5. He made a delicious apple pie for **desert**.
6. Good we have her on board. She's an **engaged** member of the team.
7. These components are produced in our **fabric** in Poland.
8. Be careful, some mushrooms contain **gift**.
9. The children will be sent to **gymnasium** next year.
10. I couldn't do without my **handy** any more, not even for a day.
11. She studies the degree program entitled "Digital Economy" at a **high school** in Berlin.
12. This is a difficult question. I'd like to hear what you **mean**.

13. A lot of **mobbing** is going on in schools these days.
14. Have you been to the **oldtimer** show yet? Lots of fascinating vehicles there!
15. There are too many items on the agenda. **Eventually** we need a follow-up meeting soon.
16. His arguments were **pregnant**, simple, and clear.
17. If I'd known he was so **sensible**, I wouldn't have teased him.
18. Don't carry too many glasses on your **tablet**. It's risky!
19. They've developed a brand-new software **technique** in the start-up company.
20. Have you been to Macy's in New York yet? They say it's one of the world's largest **warehouses**.

11 Interkulturelle Hinweise [Some Intercultural Communication Tips]

Bitte bedenken Sie: Das Verhalten von Geschäftspartnern aus anderen Ländern ist (wie Ihr eigenes) sowohl soziokulturell als auch individuell geprägt. Daher ist Vorsicht geboten: Schließen Sie nicht von dem, was Sie in einer Begegnung erleben, auf die Gesamtheit der ausländischen Partner oder gar auf die Nation. Lassen Sie neue Eindrücke in Ruhe auf sich wirken, hören Sie zu, schauen Sie sich um, agieren Sie bedächtig: Ihr Geschäftspartner wird es honorieren. Dafür gibt es im Englischen übrigens ein sehr passendes Sprichwort: „When in Rome, do as the Romans do".

Wir gehen im Folgenden besonders auf Großbritannien und die Vereinigten Staaten als bedeutende englischsprachige Wirtschaftsregionen ein; bedenken Sie aber, dass Englisch in mindestens 75 Staaten der Welt Amtssprache ist oder einen besonderen Status hat; das entspricht einer Bevölkerung von über zwei Milliarden.[1]

11.1 Großbritannien

In Geschäftsbeziehungen mit britischen Partnern beachten Sie bitte folgende Besonderheiten:

- „Small Talk" zu Beginn einer Verhandlung spielt eine wichtige Rolle. Sie sprechen über belanglose Themen wie z. B. Ihre Anreise oder das Wetter, das Eis ist nach einer solchen Phase schnell gebrochen und die Stimmung für das bevorstehende Treffen positiv. Vermeiden Sie politische oder zu persönliche Themen.
- „Handshaking": Im englischsprachigen Sprachraum geben Sie sich beim ersten Kennenlernen und oft bei einem Wiedersehen nach längerer Zeit die Hand. Im täglichen Umgang ist das Händeschütteln unüblich.
- Sitzungen beginnen – wie in Deutschland – stets pünktlich, planen Sie daher Ihre Anreise sorgfältig.
- In der englischsprachigen Welt reden sich Geschäftspartner schon nach einem ersten kurzen Austausch mit dem Vornamen

an. Wenn Sie aber unsicher sind, warten Sie am besten, bis Sie dazu aufgefordert werden („Please call me Rob").

- Die englische Verhandlungssprache ist sehr höflich, positiv und diplomatisch. So genannte „downtoners" (Wörter, die eine Aussage abschwächen) sind weit verbreitet (z. B. „perhaps", „slightly"), um zurückhaltend zu agieren. Eine zu direkte Argumentation wird häufig als unhöflich empfunden.
- Akademische Titel (Dr.) sind der Wissenschaft vorbehalten und werden in Gesprächen nicht benutzt (außer im Kontakt mit Ärzten).

11.2 Vereinigte Staaten von Amerika

Viele Tipps für den Umgang mit britischen Geschäftspartnern gelten auch für die Vereinigte Staaten. Einige Besonderheiten kommen hinzu:

- Amerikanische Geschäftspartner sind direkter in der Kommunikation. Klarheit, Logik und Gradlinigkeit werden geschätzt und Formalitäten nachgeordnet, denn: „Time is money". „Beating around the bush" (um den heißen Brei herumreden) ist nicht angesagt, stattdessen kommen die Partner schnell zum Punkt („get down to business"). Entsprechend kürzer fällt der Small Talk aus.
- Wundern Sie sich nicht, wenn persönliche Dinge zur Sprache kommen. Erlebnisse aus der Familie werden gerne geschildert. Bereiten Sie sich darauf vor, dass Sie auch über ein persönliches Detail sprechen. Dies kann durchaus als Eisbrecher wirken.
- Der Umgang mit amerikanischen Partnern ist tendenziell unkompliziert. Sie sind in der Regel offen und risikobereit. Ihnen geht es um die Aufgabe, die erfolgreich zu erledigen ist, weniger um die persönlichen Beziehungen. In diesem Zusammenhang wird oft die Aussage des früheren amerikanischen Präsidenten Calvin Coolidge (1872–1933) zitiert: „The chief business of the American people is business."
- Die Angewohnheit, elektronische Geräte wie Smartphones während der Verhandlungen zu nutzen, wirkt bei amerikanischen

Geschäftspartnern grob unhöflich und sollte daher vermieden werden.

- Gastgeschenke sind im geschäftlichen Kontext unerwünscht, die Compliance-Regeln vieler Firmen verbieten dies sogar ausdrücklich.

11.3 Lingua franca – non-native speakers

- Das British Council und die Bundeszentrale für politische Bildung[1] haben interessante Fakten zusammengetragen, die die Bedeutung des Englischen unterstreichen. Experten schätzen, dass um das Jahr 2020 etwa zwei Milliarden Menschen, also rund ein Viertel der Weltbevölkerung, Alltagsenglisch ("English at a useful level") beherrschen. Englisch ist unangefochten die Sprache der Wissenschaft, der IT, des Handels, der Unterhaltung und der Diplomatie. Rund 350 Millionen Menschen sprechen Englisch als Muttersprache, etwa 600 Millionen als Zweitsprache; hinzu kommen rund 750 Millionen Menschen, für die Englisch Fremdsprache ist.
- Die englische Sprache hat sich nach dem Zweiten Weltkrieg und vor allem in den letzten 20 Jahren, begünstigt durch die rasante Verbreitung der neuen Medien, zur wichtigsten internationalen Verkehrssprache entwickelt, auch als Lingua franca bezeichnet.
- Englisch als Lingua franca ist nicht grundsätzlich anders als das Englisch, das von Muttersprachlern weltweit gesprochen wird. Eine Ausnahme stellt die Aussprache dar: Neben den ohnehin vorhandenen muttersprachlichen Färbungen kommen in der Verkehrssprache Englisch noch einmal zahlreiche Aussprachevarianten hinzu, die aber zu keinen gravierenden Kommunikationsproblemen führen sollten. Und: Stellen Sie sich darauf ein, dass sich die Sprachkompetenz der einzelnen Sprecher stark unterscheiden kann.
- Englisch als Lingua franca hat auch eine einende Funktion: nicht in kultureller Hinsicht, sondern unter dem Gesichtspunkt, Kommunikation grenzübergreifend möglich zu machen.

- Gepflogenheiten aus dem Umgang mit englischen oder amerikanischen Partnern werden zunehmend auf Verhandlungen mit Nicht-Muttersprachlern übertragen. So findet der unkomplizierte Gebrauch des Vornamens auch zwischen europäischen Partnern insgesamt verstärkt Einzug.

[1] https://www.britishcouncil.org/sites/default/files/english-effect-report-v2.pdf
https://www.bpb.de/nachschlagen/zahlen-und-fakten/globalisierung/52515/weltsprache

12 Lerntipps

12.1 Die „Four Skills" beim Sprachenlernen

Beim Lernen einer Fremdsprache trainieren Sie stets vier Fertigkeiten: das Hören, Sprechen, Lesen und Schreiben. Nutzen Sie jede Möglichkeit, auch nach dem Studium regelmäßig zu üben. Gelegenheit gibt es genug.

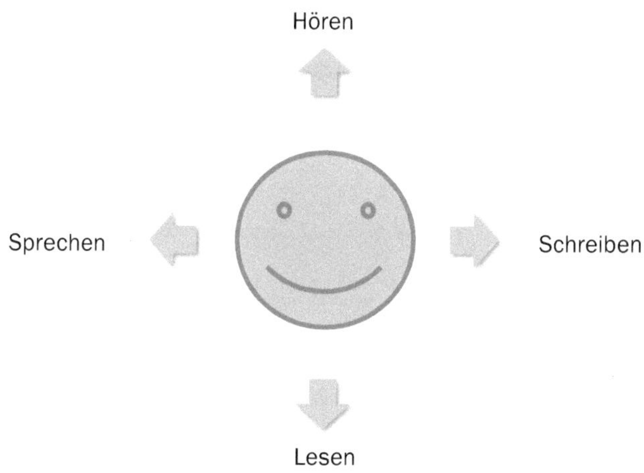

12.2 Hörverstehen

- Schauen Sie sich englischsprachige Filme oder Serien im Original an (ggf. mit Untertiteln), entweder im Kino oder auf DVD, gerne auch im Internet. Es gibt zudem fesselnde Serien bei den Streaming-Diensten. Persönliche Empfehlungen des Autors: „The Crown" (Netflix) und „The Marvelous Mrs. Maisel" (Amazon Prime).
- Schalten Sie regelmäßig englische Radiosender ein; Nachrichtensendungen z. B. sind recht gut zu verstehen, weil Sie den Kontext (das, worum es geht) gut einordnen können, denn Sie hören / sehen ja auch deutsche Nachrichten. Auch Podcasts sind gut geeignet, z. B. „The Inquiry" von der BBC, wo sich die Folgen mit

aktuellen politischen bzw. sozialen Fragestellungen beschäftigen (https://www.bbc.co.uk/programmes/p029399x).

- Hörbücher oder „Audio Books“ sind attraktiv: Sie bieten Ihnen authentische Sprache verbunden mit Themen, die Sie wirklich interessieren. Suchen Sie sich einen Roman auf CD oder online aus, hören Sie sich ein und lassen Sie sich in die englischsprachige Welt entführen.
- Das British Council hat sehr nützliche Übungen zum Hörverstehen auf unterschiedlichen Niveaustufen zusammengestellt: https://learnenglish.britishcouncil.org/skills/listening.

12.3 Sprechen

- Nutzen Sie jede Gelegenheit, um Englisch zu sprechen: geschäftlich, im Urlaub, am Telefon usw. Keine Angst vor Fehlern, denn diese sind wichtig für den Lernprozess.
- Suchen Sie Kontakt zu Englischsprechenden, auf dem Campus, im Unternehmen, im Freundeskreis. Das müssen nicht unbedingt Muttersprachler sein, denn auch wenn Sie Englisch zur Kommunikation mit anderen Europäern, Südamerikanern oder Asiaten nutzen, machen Sie spürbar Lernfortschritte.
- Muttersprachler korrigieren, wenn Sie sie darum bitten, gerne und stets mit Taktgefühl. Profitieren Sie davon!
- Auch das Trainieren von Ausdrücken für die Geschäftswelt bietet das British Council an: https://learnenglish.britishcouncil.org/skills/speaking.

12.4 Leseverstehen

- Surfen Sie im Internet – besuchen Sie englische Seiten, die für Ihren beruflichen Kontext relevant sind, aber selbst wenn Sie „nur“ aus Spaß im Netz sind, wird das Ihre Lesekompetenz verbessern. Sehr nützliche Seite mit Leseübungen wiederum vom British Council: https://learnenglish.britishcouncil.org/skills/reading.
- Lesen Sie englische Romane / Zeitungen / Zeitschriften. Es gibt speziell auf Lerner zugeschnittene Magazine, die Vokabelerläu-

terungen und landeskundliche Zusatzinformationen enthalten (z. B. „Spotlight“, www.business-spotlight.de). Sehr zu empfehlen.

- Wenn Sie englische Texte lesen, schlagen Sie nicht jedes Wort sofort nach. Das kostet Zeit und ist frustrierend. Nutzen Sie das Wörterbuch nur, wenn Sie wirklich nicht weiterkommen, denn viele Wörter erschließen sich für Sie aus dem Zusammenhang. Sie werden sehen, nach einer Eingewöhnungszeit verstehen Sie das Gelesene recht zuverlässig. Wenn Sie sich ein „klassisches“ Wörterbuch zulegen möchten, so ist das „Langenscheidt Fachwörterbuch Kompakt Wirtschaft Englisch“ zu empfehlen, das allgemeinsprachliche Einträge und den Fachwortschatz Wirtschaft ausgewogen kombiniert.

12.5 Schreiben

- E-Mails, Kurznachrichten, Beiträge in sozialen Netzwerken auf Englisch, das alles sind gute Übungseinheiten, die Sie gar nicht als „Lernen“ wahrnehmen. Je mehr Sie schreiben, desto besser.
- Die E-Mail ist die derzeit gängigste schriftliche Kommunikationsform. Wenn Sie mit Muttersprachlern im Austausch stehen – beruflich oder privat – lassen Sie sich hin und wieder ein Feedback zu Ihrer Schreibkompetenz geben.
- Für den Hochschulbereich gibt es zahlreiche Übungsbücher zum Thema „Academic Writing“, die Sie beim Verfassen von Seminar- oder Abschlussarbeiten unterstützen.
- Sehr gute Sammlung von Schreibübungen: https://learnenglish.britishcouncil.org/skills/writing.

12.6 Wortschatz und Grammatik

Neben den kommunikativen vier Fertigkeiten sollten Sie Wert auf Wortschatz- und Grammatiktraining legen.

- Überlegen Sie sich, wie Sie persönlich Wortschatz am effektivsten lernen. Empfehlenswert ist, sich Vokabeln immer im Kontext anzueignen, also in zusammenhängenden Wortgruppen und festen Wendungen, die auch als „Wortpartner" bezeichnet werden können. Anstatt sich für das deutsche Wort „Student" nur die Übersetzung „student" einzuprägen, ist es viel sinnvoller, feste Wendungen wie „to be a first-year student, to be a law / engineering / business administration / economics student at Munich / Liverpool university" zu lernen.
- Damit wir mit Wörtern wirksam kommunizieren können, müssen sie auch regelkonform ausgesprochen werden. Gut, wenn Sie das Internationale Phonetische Alphabet (IPA) erlernt haben, mit dem die Aussprache von Wörtern beschrieben wird, zu finden in den meisten klassischen Wörterbüchern. Ein weiteres hilfreiches Instrument ist die Aussprachefunktion zahlreicher Online-Wörterbücher (z. B. www.linguee.de oder www.leo.org). Lassen Sie sich die Wörter solange vorsprechen, bis Sie sie sicher beherrschen und bei Ihrer Präsentation am nächsten Morgen souverän aussprechen können.
- Greifen Sie auf thematische Lernwortschätze zurück, die Ihnen helfen, das richtige Vokabular für die inhaltliche Vorbereitung z. B. einer Präsentation zu finden.
- Was Grammatiktraining betrifft, so gibt es hervorragende Lerngrammatiken, die sich besonders fürs Eigenstudium eignen. Sie finden Regelerklärungen, dazu passende Übungen und einen Lösungsschlüssel (z. B. die „Powergrammatik" vom Hueber Verlag). Auch im Internet finden sich viele Englisch-Portale, die kostenlos interaktive Grammatik-Übungen anbieten. Grammatik hat beim Lernen übrigens eine Hilfsfunktion, sie unterstützt die kommunikative Kompetenz, ist daher niemals Selbstzweck.

12.7 Übersetzungen

Obwohl Übersetzen eine Spezialfertigkeit ist, die einer gesonderten Ausbildung bedarf, ist es auch für den „normalen“ Sprachenanwender notwendig, einfachere und komplexe Zusammenhänge ins Englische zu übertragen (und umgekehrt). Hilfreich dabei ist nicht nur LEO (siehe oben), sondern auch http://www.linguee.de/, eine Seite, die zeigt, wie bestimmte Wörter und Sätze in der Vergangenheit übersetzt worden sind. Eine wertvolle Unterstützung, wenn auch eher für den fortgeschrittenen Anwender. Wer längere Texte übersetzen möchte, der sollte sich näher mit dem Übersetzungstool DeepL (https://www.deepl.com/translator) beschäftigen, das aus demselben Haus wie Linguee kommt. Durchaus ein ernstzunehmendes Werkzeug!

12.8 Lerntyp

In der Didaktik wird nach unterschiedlichen Lernstilen bzw. Lerntypen unterschieden. Ausschlaggebend ist dabei, welcher Wahrnehmungskanal bevorzugt wird. Die Kategorisierung nach Vester[1] ist weit verbreitet, der zwischen visuellen, auditiven und kinästhetischen bzw. haptischen Lernern / Lernerinnen differenziert. Hilfreiche Tipps, wie Sie Ihren Lerntyp näher bestimmen können, sind leicht im Internet zu finden.

1 Vester, Frederick. Denken, lernen, vergessen. Stuttgart: dva 1975.

12.9 Prüfungen

Wenn Wirtschaftsenglisch nicht Teil Ihres Studienabschlusses bzw. Ihrer beruflichen Qualifizierung ist, bietet sich für Sie ein international anerkanntes Wirtschaftsenglisch-Zertifikat an, das Ihnen bei Bewerbungsverfahren durchaus nützlich sein kann. Einen guten Überblick hat die Stiftung Warentest zusammengestellt (www.test.de/Englischzertifikate-fuer-Fortgeschrittene-Ein-Zertifikat-fuer-gutes-Englisch-4327568-0). Informieren Sie sich speziell über die Zertifikate der London Chamber of Commerce (Londoner Handelskammer, http://lccieb-germany.com/) oder die Business English Certificates der University of Cambridge (http://germany.cambridgeenglish.org/exams/bec.php). Beide Zertifikate sind international anerkannt und werden auf mehreren Kompetenzstufen angeboten.

Schlüssel zu den Übungen

Making Contacts

Exercise 1

1. pleased
2. company
3. produce
4. business
5. services
6. products
7. industry
8. colleague
9. introduce
10. self-employed

Exercise 2

The correct matching is 1 f, 2 h, 3 i, 4 c, 5 d, 6 g, 7 a, 8 e, 9 j, 10 b.

Exercise 3

1. Did you find your way here alright?
2. What would you like to drink?
3. Is this your first time in Berlin?
4. Will you have any time to look around Berlin?
5. Shall we get down to business?

Talking about Companies, Products and Services

Exercise 1

1. I'm in charge
2. deal with
3. I'm involved
4. purchasing department, buy / purchase

Exercise 2

2. special
   specialist (n.)
   specialization (n.)
   speciality (n.)
   to specialize in sthg. (v.)
   special (adj.)
   specialized (adj., eg. staff)
   specially (adv.)

3. Employment
   employment (n.)
   employer (n.)
   employee (n.)
   to employ (v., staff)

4. Innovation
   innovation (n.)
   innovator (n.)
   innovative (adj.)
   to innovate (v.)

Exercise 3

The correct matching is 1 d, 2 e, 3 f, 4 c, 5 a, 6 g, 7 b.

Telephoning in English

Exercise 1

1. Good morning, ABC Ltd., how can I help you?
2. Who's calling please?
3. Could I speak to Miriam Mind please?
4. I'll put you through.
5. I'm sorry. Ms Mind is in a meeting right now.
6. Can I take a message for her?
7. Thanks for calling. Goodbye.

Exercise 2

Receptionist	**Caller**
1. Good afternoon, Master-Mind Ltd. Can I help you?	2. Yes, I'd like to speak to Chris Clever if he's available.
3. I'm sorry. Mr Clever is out of the office at the moment. Would you like to leave a message?	4. Yes. I'm Duncan Dumble, please tell him to call me back. It's quite urgent.
5. I'm sorry, I didn't catch your last name. Could you spell it for me please?	6. Yes of course. It's D-U-M-B-L-E.
7. OK Mr Dumble. I will tell him as soon as he returns.	8. Thank you very much. Goodbye.
9. Thank you for calling and have a nice day.	

Exercise 3

1. Q.: Can I help you?
2. Q.: Who's calling, please?
3. Q.: What can I do for you?
4. Q.: I'd like to speak to Alan, please.
5. Q.: The line's bad. Could you speak up please?

Writing Business Letters and E-Mails

Exercise 1

1. Dear Ms Miller is best because Ms is the standard form of address used for female business partners.
2. The correct order is a, b, d, c, f, e.
3. Forms like "I'll, I'm, I won't" are used in e-mails or spoken language, not in business letters.
4. False.
5. In e-mails you can use the bcc function if you want to send e-mails to a list of multiple recipients and privacy is an important issue. Or your line manager / colleague wants to be updated about an email conversation with a customer, but without their knowledge.

Exercise 2

Hi Maria
Concerning the data that is still missing, I've now put everything together and will upload the file later today. Can you please confirm whether, in spite of the delay, you can still finish the program on time?
I'm sorry about the delay. Thanks for your support in this matter.
Hope to hear from you soon.
Kind regards
Chris

Exercise 3

The correct matching is: 1 e, 2 c, 3 a, 4 f, 5 b, 6 d.

Discussing Graphs

Exercise 1

1 rise 2 fall 3 fluctuate 4 peak 5 bottom out 6 recover 7 level off

Exercise 2

1 fluctuate / go up and down 2 rise / go up / increase / grow
3 go down / fall / decrease / drop 4 level off / stabilize / stay the same

Exercise 3

1. At first, sales rose rapidly and peaked / reached a peak.
2. Then sales showed a dramatic / pronounced decrease / bottomed out / reached a low point.
3. In the following period, there was a significant increase / upturn in sales.
4. After that, sales fluctuated / went up and down for some time.
5. Sales levelled off / stabilized / stayed the same in the final period.

Exercise 4

1. Household appliances represent 35 % of sales.
2. Consumer electronics account for 40 % of sales.
3. Cameras and electronic equipment make up 25 % of sales.

Negotiating in English

Exercise 1

1. agenda
2. get down to
3. contract
4. difference
5. profit
6. payment

7. requirements
8. summary

Exercise 2

Dear Richard / Dear Josephine

It was good to meet you again and discuss the new deal with you. Let me briefly summarize the results of our discussion.

First, we agreed to the specifications of the metal chair. Please check the enclosed documents for details.
We further agreed that you will supply 15,000 chairs in the first and 20,000 chairs in the second year. After that, we will re-negotiate the quantities / discuss the quantities again.
The wholesale price per unit will be 75 €.
Delivery is to commence / will start not later than 4 months from now, since we need the chairs promptly for the summer season.

Thanks again for the fruitful meeting. I very much look forward to doing business with you.

Kind regards
XXX

Exercise 3

The correct order is 1 f, 2 g, 3 h, 4 e, 5 b, 6 a, 7 c, 8 d.

Presenting in English

Exercise 1

The correct order is 3, 6, 1, 2, 5, 4.

Exercise 2

Greeting the audience/ Introducing yourself	Introducing the topic	Moving from one point to the next	Referring to something said before/ dealing with questions	Introducing contrasting arguments	Summarizing the results of your presentation
Good morning, colleagues. My name is ...	I've divided my talk into three main parts. In my presentation I'm going to explain ...	Now let's move on to ... The next point I'd like to make is ...	As I've already mentioned ... Can we get back to this a bit later?	However, ... On the other hand, ...	If I may recap the most important points. Let me summarize the main points.

Exercise 3

1. False. It is the other way round.
2. False. This would bore your audience. Use the slides (with key points only) to illustrate your main arguments and speak freely.
3. True. This will help you gain confidence.
4. True. These are important tools to focus the audience's attention.
5. False. Be there well in advance and make yourself familiar with the venue and test the technical equipment.

Chairing a Meeting

Exercise 1

1. agenda
2. minutes
3. objective
4. attending
5. chair
6. the floor is yours
7. off-topic
8. Any Other Business

Exercise 2

The correct order is 6, 3, 4, 2, 1, 5.

Exercise 3

1. attention
2. purpose
3. campaign
4. item
5. schedule
6. comment
7. wrap up
8. recap
9. summarize
10. cover

Applying for a Job in English

Exercise 1

1. experience
2. employed, Product Manager
3. excellent skills
4. independent, team player

Exercise 2

1. in charge
2. running / supervising
3. negotiating
4. forwarding
5. writing
6. reducing
7. increasing, 10 %
8. obtaining

Exercise 3

1. part
2. planned / organised / prepared
3. developed / designed
4. expanded

Exercise 4

1. skills
2. extensive / comprehensive
3. C1
4. available, request

False Friends

	Wrong word	Correct option
1	actual: wirklich, tatsächlich	aktuell: current, topical
2	beamer: BMW (Automarke, BE)	Beamer: data projector
3	chef: Küchenchef	Chef: boss
4	to control: regulieren, steuern	kontrollieren: to check, to monitor
5	desert /ˈdezət/: Wüste	Dessert: dessert /dɪˈzɜːt/
6	engaged: verlobt, besetzt	engagiert: committed
7	fabric: Stoff	Fabrik: factory
8	gift: Geschenk	Gift: poison
9	gymnasium: Turnhalle	Gymnasium: grammar school BE, high school AE
10	handy: praktisch, handlich	Handy: mobile phone BE, cell phone AE
11	high school: Sekundarstufe	Hochschule: college, university
12	to mean: bedeuten	meinen: to think
13	to mob: umringen, umlagern	mobben: to bully
14	oldtimer: Veteran	Oldtimer: vintage car BE, classic car AE/BE
15	eventually: schließlich, letztendlich	eventuell: possibly, perhaps
16	pregnant: schwanger	prägnant: concise
17	sensible: vernünftig	sensibel: sensitive
18	tablet: Tablette, Tablet-Computer	Tablett: tray

19	technique: Technik, Methode, Technik	Technologie: technology
20	warehouse: Lager	Warenhaus: department store

Ein **Tipp zum Schluss**: Versuchen Sie, während des Studiums oder in den ersten Jahren Ihres Berufslebens für einige Monate ins (englischsprachige) Ausland zu gehen. Es gibt keine bessere Möglichkeit, sich sprachlich rasch weiterzuentwickeln, interkulturell an Erfahrungen zu gewinnen und dabei gleichzeitig Freude zu haben. Sie werden nachhaltig davon profitieren.

Viel Erfolg beim Lernen!

Hilfreiche Materialien fürs Englischlernen: eine Auswahlbibliographie

Allgemeine Wörterbücher und Fachwörterbücher (zweisprachig)

Langenscheidt-Collins Großwörterbuch Englisch. München und Glasgow: Langenscheidt-Collins 2019.

Langenscheidt Fachwörterbuch Kompakt Wirtschaft Englisch. München: Langenscheidt 2012.

Langenscheidt Fachwörterbuch Kompakt Technik Englisch. München: Langenscheidt 2012.

PONS Wörterbuch Schule und Studium 1: Englisch-Deutsch. Stuttgart: Pons 2016.

PONS Wörterbuch Schule und Studium 2: Deutsch-Englisch. Stuttgart: Pons 2016.

Einsprachige Wörterbücher

Advanced Learners' Dictionary. Berlin: Cornelsen 2020.

Dictionary of Contemporary English – DCE. München: Langenscheidt 2016.

Macmillan English Dictionary for Advanced Learners. München: Hueber 2013.

Wortschatz

Baddock, Barry; Vrobel, Susie: Großer Lernwortschatz Wirtschaftsenglisch aktuell. München: Hueber 2013

Emmerson, Paul: Business Vocabulary Builder. The words and phrases you need to succeed. Oxford: Macmillan 2015.

Hoffmann, Hans G.; Hoffmann, Marion: Großer Lernwortschatz Englisch aktuell. München: Hueber 2013.

MacCarthy, Michael; O'Dell, Felicity: English Collocations in Use – Intermediate. Cambridge: CUP: 2017.

Mascull, Bill: Business Vocabulary in Use – Intermediate. Cambridge: CUP 2010.

Übungsmaterialien

Emmerson, Paul: Email English 2nd edition. Oxford: Macmillan 2013.

Hughes, John: Telephone English. Oxford: Macmillan 2006

Stevens, John: Englisch einfach richtig. Typische Fehler vermeiden. München: Hueber 2019.

Hoffmann, Hans G.; Hoffmann, Marion: Großes Übungsbuch Englisch neu. Grammatik. München: Hueber 2014

Williams, Erica J.: Presentations in English. Find your voice as a presenter. Oxford: Macmillan 2008.

Grammatik

Duckworth, Michael: Essential Business Grammar and Practice. Oxford: OUP 2006.

Emmerson, Paul: Essential Business Grammar Builder. Oxford: Macmillan 2006.

Emmerson, Paul: Business Grammar Builder: Second Edition – Intermediate to Upper-Intermediate. Oxford: Macmillan 2010.

Hoffmann, Hans G.; Hoffmann, Marion: Große Lerngrammatik Englisch – Vollständige Neubearbeitung. Regeln, Anwendungsbeispiele, Tests. München: Hueber 2010.

MacCarthy, Michael; McCarten, Jeanne; Clark, David; Clark, Rachel: Grammar for Business with Audio CD. Cambridge: CUP 2009.

Murphy, Raymond: English Grammar in Use with Answers and CD-ROM: A Self-study Reference and Practice Book for Intermediate Learners of English. Cambridge: CUP 2019.

Stevens, John: Business Grammar – no problem. Eine Englischgrammatik mit Übungen und Tests. Berlin: Cornelsen 2010.

Stevens, John: Die neue Powergrammatik Englisch. Für Anfänger zum Üben und Nachschlagen. München: Hueber 2017.

Walther, Lutz. Langenscheidt Komplett-Grammatik Englisch. Das Standardwerk zum Nachschlagen und Trainieren. München: Langenscheidt 2015.

TOEFL (Test of English as a Foreign Language) Vorbereitung

Sharpe, Pamela: Barron's TOEFL IBT – Internet-Based Test. New York: Barron's Educational Series 2016.

Bewerben auf Englisch

Pocklington, Jackie; Schulz; Patrik; Zettl, Erich. Bewerben auf Englisch. Leitfaden mit Tipps und Mustern. Berlin: Cornelsen 2010.
Pocklington, Jackie, "The Key to Designing Successful Job Applications". https://www.fu-berlin.de/sites/career/_ressourcen/Internationales_Ressourcen/Key-to-Designing-Job-Application.pdf.

Stichwortverzeichnis